HEALING OILS

Healing Oils

Roxane Harper

Unless otherwise indicated, all Scripture quotations are taken from the *King James Version* of the Bible.

Scriptures quotations marked TLB are taken from *The Living Bible*.

Healing Oils
ISBN 978-0-9817358-0-1
Copyright © 2005 by Roxane Harper

Library of Congress 2008927769

Front Cover illustration by Cathi Stevenson
Book Cover image by Emin Ozkan

CONTENTS

DEDICATION

THIS book is dedicated to the Lord of our Healing the Great Physician, Jesus Christ.

ACKNOWLEDGEMENTS

I give all glory to our Lord and Savior Jesus Christ for loving us enough to heal us. This book is dedicated to the memory of my dear friend Judy and to my God Daughter, Charity. Thank you for the original cover design. Jesus loves you so much.

To the person that runs things, and one of the sweetest daughters ever, Qiava. Key-Key you saw this book in me and pushed hard to get it out. I give special love and acknowledgements to the most wonderful husband in the world, to my children and my children's children for making me laugh and loving me.

I thank God for Mike and Johnny Robinson of the UGMX Studios in San Jose, California for all their work on the audio book. These guys are a blessing from God. Special thanks to my God Son, Xavier Dotson aka "Zatoven" for making beautiful music on the audio book. I love you Zay! Lastly, I would like to pronounce God's blessings on the JCFANS, for always pulling on the anointing for miracles.

THOUGHTS ON "HEALING OILS"

Cancer Patients Believe

I am truly grateful to God for bringing Pastor Roxane Harper into my life. She is an anointed woman of God who fervently seeks after Him. She is also an extraordinary preacher and teacher. Her powerful message in "Healing Oils" will minister to each person who reads it whether they are seeking healing for themselves or for a loved one.

I believe God puts people into our lives for special reasons. I met Pastors Willie and Roxane Harper in late 2005. My husband and I were leasing a large facility on Mars Way in Tracy, California where we ran fitness boot camps and offered personal training. Each month we struggled to pay our rent, but we were determined to make the business work. We thought if we could share the space with another business, we might be able to make the lease payments each month. My good friend introduced us to the Harpers and told us they were looking for a place in which to expand their church, Jesus Christ for All Nations (JCFANS), into Tracy. At the same time, we were also looking for a church home.

The Harpers were very gracious and welcoming. They invited us into their home, their lives, and their ministry. In mid-2006 JCFANS-Tracy officially moved into our building. While we had done our best to make the place look nice, we had no heating or air conditioning, and we had no carpet. We wondered from time to time why we faithfully attended church every Sunday in an uncomfortable building where it was either freezing cold or blazing hot. But God knew why and he had a plan.

When I was diagnosed with breast cancer at the age of 32, one of the first people I called was Pastor Roxane. I knew she had been healed of breast cancer right before I met her and I looked to her for comfort and direction. God built our relationship during our time together in the Mars Way building knowing that one day I would need her strength and prayers to get me through a tough time.

On May 2nd 2008 my tough time came. While many women survive breast cancer every year, the doctors told me I had an advanced stage of cancer and there was a high probability the cancer had spread to other parts of my body. My oncologist told me that if the cancer had spread, they would give me one to two years to live. I needed Pastor Roxane's strength, so I went to her.

As I sat in her kitchen early one morning in prayer, I was filled with the Holy Spirit and began speaking in tongues for the first time. God spoke into my spirit and said "Joleen, you are either going to be hot or cold for me, choose now which one it's going to be." I chose to be hot for Him and to believe that my work on this earth was not finished.

I have not looked back since that day. As I went through my treatment and through days of uncertainty, I did not know the direction the Lord was taking me. I read "Healing Oils" and I was extremely blessed by the book. There were many times I felt her words reflected my own specific thoughts and feelings. It was as if she wrote the book predicting exactly what my fears and emotions would be.

Pastor Roxane writes about the fear we have of knowing God can heal you, but not knowing if he wants to; wondering why God wants to take your life when you haven't yet left your mark on the world; and taking your place at the front of the line for the trials of life.

To anyone who is going through an illness and is seeking healing, this book will lift your spirits and help you unlock the healing power of

God. The God of the Bible is still performing miracles today, you just have to keep your eyes on Jesus and believe that he wants to heal you.

"I have told you these things so that in me you may have peace. In this world you will have trouble. But take heart! I have overcome the world."
John 16:33 (NIV)

One week after I was told there was no hope for me if the cancer had spread; I had a PET and CT Scan. As I lay in the machine, God told me my scan would come back clean. Since God is always true to His word, my doctor called two days later and told me the scan did not show any cancer in my body.

I thank God for Pastor Roxane. She is a wonderful woman of God who is ***CRAAAZY*** for Jesus. She helped me believe in God's healing power and to regain my fire for Jesus. Through this book, you will have a piece of her strength, power and wisdom. I hope this book is as much of a blessing to you as it has been for me.

In Him,

Joleen Ruffin
Cancer Survivor

FOREWORD

"HEALING OILS"

My life has been profoundly impacted by Roxane Harper. She is a wife, mother, evangelist, pastor, teacher, counselor, real estate broker, healer, and now author. This book is just a sampling of how God is using her to illustrate that just a simple act of faith can turn what Satan wants as your greatest defeat into your greatest triumph.

In the book "Healing Oils" Roxane shows you how to expand your capacity to believe God for your healing. In other words, you need to have a strong relationship with Jesus first before you can be assured of what you ask for. That is, to look into the face of God and see him as he reveals himself. Later, when you face what seems like your biggest fear, you will still see the face of God and have faith. She acknowledges that it is not easy, but through her personal testing she challenges you to be obedient to God and watch Him move you to the "front of the line".

I am particularly impressed with the manner in which Roxane builds your faith in her own example by courageously trusting God more than the doctors. She leads you to his special touch in your life while assuring you that Jesus is always with you. As she directs you in praying the prayer of faith in your own life, you will develop the strength to hold fast in the midst of difficult circumstances.

Finally, Roxane does not see her personal healing as an exception, but rather a prescription of what God can do for anybody who seeks his face, follows his word, and applies it faithfully.

Dr. Bruce S. Riley, MFT
Pastor / Marriage and Family Therapist

INTRODUCTION

HEALING OILS

The Prescription for God's Healing Power

He sent his word, and healed them, and delivered them from their destructions.

Ps 107:20

THE God of all the earth sent His word to heal and rescue us from sickness and disease. Jesus has the cure for all diseases and is ready to freely share it with all who believe. The Lord Jesus Christ has a healing flow that will heal any infirmity that holds His people in bondage. The idea of divine intervention in the health of the believers in Jesus Christ has been a reality for centuries, and remains a reality today. An account in the book of Exodus declares that God has the ability to prevent and destroy all diseases that might plague human kind. He cried out to the children of Israel *"for I am the Lord that healeth thee"* because healing truly belongs to God and flows from His presence.

And said, If thou wilt diligently hearken to the voice of the LORD thy God, and wilt do that which is right in his sight, and wilt give ear to his commandments, and keep all his statutes, I will put none of these diseases upon thee, which I have brought upon the Egyptians: for I am the LORD that healeth thee.

Ex 15:26

This healing power of the Lord belongs to His children and He takes delight in the health and prosperity of His people. Jesus Himself suffered pain, shame, death and was beaten so we could be healed. His sacrifice resulted in our new testament benefit package which includes access to God's divine healing power.

Bless the LORD, O my soul, and forget not all his benefits: Who forgiveth all thine iniquities; who healeth all thy diseases;

Ps 103:2-3

For many years I knew this to be possible intellectually, but I have now personally experienced the healing power of God. You see, Jesus healed me of breast cancer without any natural intervention or treatment and I will never be the same again. The joy that comes with God's healing touch is an indescribable life changing event that pushes us into another realm of glory. Our Lord Jesus declared in His word that healing is the "children's bread" which means that we have an inherited right to receive divine healing if we walk in covenant with Him.

But Jesus said unto her, Let the children first be filled: for it is not meet to take the children's bread, and to cast it unto the dogs.

Mark 7:27

In that same verse, Mark 7:27 Jesus was speaking to a Gentile woman who had requested healing for her child. His reply to her gives us great insight into healing as a new covenant benefit since he declared that healing was the bread of His children. At this point in the earthly ministry of Jesus He was only revealing Himself to the Jewish people and had not opened the way of salvation to the Gentiles. He proclaimed that the children should first be filled, indicating that this benefit was to be given to those in His family first. It is imperative that we enter the family of God to be assured that He will help us in our time of need. The healing oils of God flow from the veins of our savior and are extended to whosoever will believe and receive Him.

Therefore it is with extreme excitement that I have decided to embark upon this writing because my heart is bleeding for the people of God along with all who do not know him in His healing power. I am yearning for a move of God that will cause this generation to realize that the Lord Jesus Christ is in control of every aspect of our lives. I do not consider myself a great theologian, but I have an earnest desire to minister hope to every seemingly ordinary person that is struggling to believe that God has a miracle for them.

There are numerous great men and women in the body of Christ that would be better qualified to undertake this project, but the spirit of God has pressed my spirit for some time to offer a work that would allow his healing nature to flow from its pages to the countless multitudes in sick beds and hospitals throughout this world that are longing for answers and a healing touch from God. There have been many notable works written that could easily minister and have ministered to many, but I have felt the call of God to write to every man, woman, boy and girl that has lost hope and longs for the flame of God to be ignited in their spirit causing the "Healing Oils" from God to flow into their lives. Many that read these pages will be instantly healed because they believe what is written and by doing so their faith will touch the faith of God.

The motivation for this book started many years ago when I set at the bedside of a dear friend that was suffering with cancer. In spite of all my hopefulness and prayers, she died. The doctors did their very best to relieve her of the disease but all their efforts failed. At that point I realized that doctors are fallible but God is infallible. Her death left me sad, confused, and with an unquenchable thirst and desire to minister to anyone that would hear and believe that "God wants to heal them". This Book is called "Healing Oils" because there is an anointed flow of supernatural oil that emanates from the Lord Jesus Christ bringing healing to our bodies and souls. In the Old Testament the people of God would utilize a balm that was produced in the region of Gilead as a medicinal ointment for the healing of wounds. There is a spiritual parallel to every natural occurrence in this life, which causes us to see that true healing comes from the spirit of God. No ointment or physician can do what Jesus can, which is to completely eradicate sickness and disease. It is not our intention to bring an indictment against physicians or medical institutions because they have their place in the grand scheme of things. Yes, physicians receive their knowledge and ability from God, therefore their work is good, but inevitably there will come a time when the gifts of the physician are not adequate to relieve our feeble bodies of the pain and suffering of sickness and disease. The time will come when we must seek the wisdom and healing power of God before we consider any other alternative. Jesus wants to be first in our life while receiving our total devotion.

King Asa, a king of Judah, died with a disease because he trusted the physicians more than he trusted God. "And Asa in the thirty and ninth year of his reign was diseased in his feet, until his disease was exceeding great: yet in his disease he sought not to the LORD, but to the physicians. And Asa slept with his fathers, and died in the one and fortieth year of his reign."

> *"In the thirty-ninth year of his reign, Asa became seriously diseased in his feet, but he didn't go to the Lord with the problem but to the doctors."*
>
> *2 Chron 16:12-13 (TLB)*

I am not saying that we will never get sick or die, but when our back is up against the wall and all the medicine and treatments have failed, Jesus will manifest His Healing flow. There is a work of faith that will help us tap into the oil that flows from the throne of God. If you are sick Jesus wants to heal you. If you have lost all hope because of what you are going through, Jesus wants to heal you. His love for you is so great that He cannot bear to see you sick. I know that this is hard to believe at times because of the severity of what we go through but our Father does not receive any glory in the sickness of His people.

As you continue to read the pages of this book please take some time alone to pray and worship as you are led by God. We have included prayers at the end of each chapter as a guideline and springboard to help facilitate your time with the Father. Do not limit yourself to the written prayers but allow God to put words in your heart that you can speak to Him. Try praying until your heart is full. In addition, we will be looking at the historical account of a woman in the Bible that had a physical ailment in her body for twelve years. This woman's story will be used as a backdrop for the presentation of truths that we will discuss in this book. This unknown woman will help us to see an example of the kind of faith that really moves God into action. Please read on to discover God's Prescription for His Healing Power and prepare to receive your miracle of healing.

Father,
I feel the beginning of something wonderful taking place in my life and desire to hear your voice as I access your healing power. Lord share the oil of your Healing Flow with me and bring me into the benefits of your covenant. I have been helpless and hopeless for so long but suddenly I feel an amazing excitement about my future. Open my heart that I might understand and receive your word of healing. You sent your word to heal me and I am ready to receive from you.

CHAPTER 1

WHERE IS GOD?

Is there no medicine in Gilead? Is there no physician there? Why doesn't God do something? Why doesn't he help?

Jer 8:22 TLB

THE question of where God is in times of trouble and suffering has been asked many times. When we or someone we love is sick it turns our life upside down. This is a time of suffering like none other. When our body is weak it affects everything else about us. Our daily schedule is changed, our mental capacity is diminished, our work goes undone and the lives of our family and friends are disrupted.

Questions enter our mind during times of sickness and distress: Why does God allow sickness? Can he really heal us? How long will our suffering last? Is it really His will to heal us? What do I have to do to receive His healing mercies? Is healing just for others? Does God even care? Is it my purpose to suffer? These same questions have been asked for centuries, even in the Bible days. The prophet Jeremiah caused Israel to ponder the question when he asked them in the book of Jeremiah "Is there no medicine in Gilead? Is there no physician there? Why doesn't God do something? Why doesn't he help?" Even though Jeremiah was not talking to Israel about physical sickness the same answers apply. Whether we are oppressed by sickness in our bodies or because of the spiritual sickness of our nation the "Healing Oils" of God succeed when applied to our life.

God Does Not Forget

Solomon gave us a depiction of unrequited love in the Song of Solomon. The love of his life was gone and he could not find her. One of the worst feelings in life is the longing for someone that you love that has gone away. As we suffer the trials of this life there is a deep longing for someone outside ourselves to help us and when it doesn't happen it leaves us empty and alone.

I opened to my beloved; but my beloved had withdrawn himself, and was gone: my soul failed when he spake: I sought him, but I could not find him; I called him, but he gave me no answer.

Song of Solomon 5:6

The scriptures also tell us that when the thing that we hope for is put on hold our heart becomes ill.

Hope deferred makes the heart sick; but when dreams come true at last, there is life and joy.

Prov 13:12 (TLB)

The Lord does not take pleasure in making us wait in pain and agony. If you, or someone close to you is experiencing some type of sickness or physical difficulty this book is for you. Just imagine a mother sitting helplessly at the bedside of a sick child and you might begin to understand how God feels about your illness. The scripture says:

"Can a woman forget her sucking child, that she should not have compassion on the son of her womb? yea, they may forget, yet will I not forget thee."

Isa 49:15

The Living version expresses it like this:

"Can a mother forget her little child and not have love for her own son? Yet even if that should be; I will not forget you."

Isa 49:15

God said **never**!!! If a natural mother cannot forget her little child God cannot forget you. We are forever on the mind of the Lord. Natural parents may disappoint us and even abandon us but Jesus cannot forget us and will never leave us.

for he hath said, I will never leave thee, nor forsake thee. So that we may boldly say, The Lord is my helper, and I will not fear what man shall do unto me.

Heb 13:5-6

The Lord is with us in our trials and tribulations; He will never leave us to go it alone. He said that He would never leave us or forsake us for any reason. The latter clause of the scripture expresses His desire for us to be bold in our declaration of faith as we trust in His power to deliver us in adverse situations.

"That is why we can say without any doubt or fear, "The Lord is my Helper, and I am not afraid of anything that mere man can do to me."

Heb 13:6 (TLB)

We are on his mind and in his heart. The love that God has for his people is stronger than that which is produced in a natural relationship.

One of the deepest relationships in life is the love of a mother for her infant child. We make adjustments to our entire life surrounding the care of the new creation that God has given us. It is utterly unthinkable for a mother to be unmindful of that tie, or to forsake the child that she loves. She will succor it in times of sickness and distress and she would never watch it suffer without any attempt to relieve its pain. The psalmist tells us that God is a father that pities His children when they love him.

> *"He is like a father to us, tender and sympathetic to those who reverence him."*
>
> *Ps 103:13*

Webster tells us that to pity means to have sympathetic sorrow for one suffering, distressed, or unhappy. When we consider the deeper sense of the word it gives the connotation of fondling, or to love and be compassionate. God won't forget us! To forget is to be unable to think of or recall anything about a person. Forget comes from a Hebrew root word that means to mislay, or to be oblivious of, or absent from the memory or attention. Have you ever misplaced something and were unable to find it? We are God's children and we haven't been misplaced! We have not been forgotten! We are stenciled in the palm of his hand to assure His attention toward us.

> *"Behold, I have graven thee upon the palms of my hands; thy walls are continually before me."*
>
> *Isa 49:16*

What a wonderful thing to be written in God's hand where we are always before Him. It is our goal with Healing Oils to build you up in faith allowing our Lord Jesus Christ to speak to you and clearly manifest Himself through a miracle of healing. The key to hearing from God is to seek Him with our whole heart and soul. We seek Him by praying and meditating on His word. He has promised that we will find Him if we seek Him with all of our heart and with all our soul. When we find Him we will experience His healing touch.

> *But if from thence thou shalt seek the LORD thy God, thou shalt find him, if thou seek him with all thy heart and with all thy soul.*
>
> *Deut 4:29*

As we finish this chapter find a private place and pray the following prayer as you meditate on Isaiah 49:16.

Dear Heavenly Father,

You said that you would not forget me and that my name is written in the palm of your hand. I come to you today to gain strength and understanding for the problems that I am experiencing right now. I know it is not your desire to see me suffer and that you love me. Release your Healing Oils as I commit my thoughts, my body and my mind to you. Thank you for being God.

Chapter 2

A Healing Touch

"He healeth the broken in heart, and bindeth up their wounds."

Ps 147:3

JESUS is the healer of our broken hearts and our bodies. His love for us is so profound that He has given many object lessons in the scriptures to draw our attention to His divine healing ability. Jesus desires to touch us with His healing power. The Biblical account of the woman with the issue of blood is our roadmap to understanding the will of God for healing. On the way to Jairus' house to heal his twelve-year-old daughter, Jesus has an encounter with a woman who had been disabled for twelve years. In the same year that the daughter of Jairus was born a certain woman began an incredible journey of hopelessness and despair. In an awesome contrast a privileged ruler and a destitute woman both need a touch from the Master. The love of Jesus is all inclusive and embraces both male, female, rich or poor, ruler and servant. His desire is to receive our acknowledgement of His greatness by achieving what no other person can do, completely healing us.

Scientific intervention can only accomplish so much, but there are some issues that will be removed only by a touch from God. Jesus will remove, eradicate, confiscate, and do away with our problems while man can evaluate, practice and hope for the best. Remember, Jesus is the creator of all things including heaven, earth, and our bodies. Our God can do anything! He is omnipotent, omnipresent and omniscient.

He knows all, sees all, and has power over all things. One word from His mouth and cancer is obliterated, deaf ears are opened, the lame leap and the hearts of the broken are mended. He spoke the worlds into existence and His breath gave life unto men. Jeremiah spoke of His unyielding trust in God on this wise,

> *"But our refuge is your throne, eternal, high and glorious. O Lord, the Hope of Israel, all who turn away from you shall be disgraced and shamed; they are registered for earth and not for glory, for they have forsaken the Lord, the Fountain of living waters. Lord, you alone can heal me, you alone can save, and my praises are for you alone. "*
>
> *Jer 17:12-14 (TLB)*

The key to obtaining His healing touch results in acknowledging His omnipotence. We must realize that He alone is our hiding place. He is eternal and glorious, and He alone can heal and save. As a direct result of this truth it is imperative that we give our praise to Him since He alone is worthy to receive it. We live in a time where it is far more convenient to praise our doctors, our lawyers, our politicians and our own prowess, than it is to give honor and glory to the One who gives us life and breath. In most circles we have relegated Jesus to the position of a fund raiser as we give the more difficult jobs of healing and deliverance to our true heroes and idols. This in turn weakens the power of God in our life. Jesus wants all of our love, admiration and attention. He is requiring that we place the totality of our trust in Him. The word of the Lord clearly commands us to

> *"Trust in the LORD with all thine heart; and lean not unto thine own understanding."*
>
> *Prov 3:5*

When we lean on our own understanding we make the power of God in our life null and void. It is obvious that is better to put our confidence in God and not in man. Man cannot help us as we do the will of God for our lives. We must patiently trust our God that we might realize all of His promises to us. God's word says that

"It is better to trust in the LORD than to put confidence in man."
Ps 118:8

In addition, we should never stop having confidence in His ability to do what He has promised, knowing that He hears us.

"Cast not away therefore your confidence, which hath great recompence of reward."
Heb 10:35

"Do not let this happy trust in the Lord die away, no matter what happens. Remember your reward! You need to keep on patiently doing God's will if you want him to do for you all that he has promised."
Heb 10:35-36 (TLB)

"And this is the confidence that we have in him, that, if we ask any thing according to his will, he heareth us:"
1 John 5:14

He wants us to know that He is always with us. He hears us and is just waiting for us to speak to Him. Have you ever noticed when you receive bad news and are going through a struggle, that the first thing you do is stop talking and stop breathing. Think about it! We lose the ability to take deep breaths along with the ability to communicate. Well, this is the exact opposite of what God wants from us in times of crisis. In times of trouble Jesus wants us to praise Him as we rely on Him to breathe through us. The words of Job spoken in the depth of his tribulation should speak volumes to us today. While he was suffering greatly he still gave praise to God. He did not blame God for his condition nor was he angry and doubtful about the outcome, but he was resigned to trust God no matter what the circumstances.

> *"And said, Naked came I out of my mother's womb, and naked shall I return thither: the LORD gave, and the LORD hath taken away; blessed be the name of the LORD. In all this Job sinned not, nor charged God foolishly."*
>
> *Job 1:21-22*

All we need is one touch from God and a multitude of trouble will vanish. He can do anything and He specializes in the impossible. Now that you have finished this chapter close your eyes, begin to talk to the Lord Jesus about your fears, and ask for His Healing Touch. You will find that the wonders of His Healing touch are fully experienced when all of our hope is gone.

> *Dear Lord Jesus,*
> *I want so badly to believe that you will never leave me but I have felt alone for so long. I know that your word says you will never leave me but I need you to make your word a reality in my life. I am determined to touch you and am asking you to increase my faith. Thank you for your healing touch. Amen.*

CHAPTER 3

WHEN ALL HOPE IS GONE

"And a woman having an issue of blood twelve years, which had spent all her living upon physicians, neither could be healed of any,"

Luke 8:43

THE Bible talks about a certain woman who had lost all hope because she suffered with an affliction in her body for twelve years. She had a continual vaginal bleeding or hemorrhaging. It was like having a menstrual cycle for twelve years straight. This condition according to the beliefs of that time made her unclean. An unclean person was to be isolated from the people for the period of time that their bleeding continued. It had been twelve long years and there was no relief in sight for this woman which compounded her hopelessness. Anything that she set on became unclean and anyone that touched her became unclean. She had a miserable existence without the warmth of a human touch or the fellowship of a friend. She was an outcast who was left alone to deal with her condition.

"Whenever a woman menstruates, she shall be in a state of ceremonial defilement for seven days afterwards, and during that time anyone touching her shall be defiled until evening. Anything she lies on or sits on during that time shall be defiled. Anyone touching her bed or anything she sits upon shall wash his clothes and bathe himself and be ceremonially defiled until evening. A man having sexual

intercourse with her during this time is ceremonially defiled for seven days, and every bed he lies upon shall be defiled If the menstrual flow continues after the normal time, or at some irregular time during the month, the same rules apply as indicated above, so that anything she lies upon during that time is defiled, just as it would be during her normal menstrual period, and everything she sits on is in a similar state of defilement. Anyone touching her bed or anything she sits on shall be defiled, and shall wash his clothes and bathe and be defiled until evening. Seven days after the menstruating stops, she is no longer ceremonially defiled."

Lev 15:19-28 (TLB)

The very nature of her condition was causing the life source to flow out of her body. Her course was set toward death with each passing day. She was weak, frustrated, weary and broke. Many times in our life we have experienced the same dilemma that this woman confronted. At times life just doesn't work according to our plan.

"And a woman having an issue of blood twelve years, which had spent all her living upon physicians, neither could be healed of any,"

Luke 8:43

AND A WOMAN

The Bible says "and a woman". It is important that this particular woman is not identified because she could have been anyone. I believe that the importance of this scripture doesn't lie in her identity but in the fact that she comes to Jesus for relief from her troubles. The indication is that God has no respect for a man's person and that all men are important to Him. You don't have to be rich or famous to receive the benefits of God's love and grace. This woman suffered for many years and tried everything to find some relief from her condition.

In the similitude of this unknown woman there will come a point in our lives when everything around us will fail and we will be forced to also trust God. More than anything else the Lord desires our trust and confidence. This is His plan for our lives and He loves us too much to leave us in our current state.

The scriptures state that this woman spent all of her money on physicians who were unable to help her. One can only imagine the trauma and dishevelment of this woman's life. She was unable to obtain any relief from her condition and all of her resources were spent. We don't know if she had any one to turn to or if she had food or a roof over her head. We do know that she was totally desperate having lost all hope. In her desperation she came out of hiding and actively declared her utter despair in the midst of a crowd; that no doubt was threatening and may have been judgmental and hostile because of her condition. They were certainly apprehensive of being close to her for fear of becoming unclean themselves. The enemy's job is to cause us to feel alone and isolated while we experience severe challenges in our life. If he can isolate us then he can destroy us. In our isolation we cannot perceive that countless others are going through exactly the same thing that we are.

Somehow, knowing that others are experiencing similar difficulties supports the realization that the attack is not specific to us, but it is against anyone who would dare to love and seek after God. Most often we look for the enemy to destroy us in a physical way that has finality. We look for him to injure, kill or take something away from us, but the largest battle ground is for our faith in God. Yes, that's right our faith. If we lose our confidence in God we become incapacitated, hopeless, impotent and immobile. When we are immobilized we cannot fight back when our faith is under attack. We can't seem to pull ourselves out of the slump that we have fallen into. If we were truthful we would say that we feel abandoned and rejected by God. Yes, we believe in Him and love Him, but we must understand that there are times appointed to us by God Himself that are created to bring us unto perfection. He sets an appointment with us to prove our trust in and obedience to Him. It is in those times of hopelessness that Jesus loves to show His strength to those that love Him. Additionally, in these times God becomes our strength.

> *And he said unto me, My grace is sufficient for thee: for my strength is made perfect in weakness. Most gladly therefore will I rather glory in my infirmities, that the power of Christ may rest upon me.*
>
> *2 cor 12:9*

> *"For the eyes of the Lord search back and forth across the whole earth, looking for people whose hearts are perfect toward him, so that he can show his great power in helping them...."*
>
> *2 Chr 16:9 (TLB)*

WHEN THE DOCTOR CANNOT HELP

> *"And Asa in the thirty and ninth year of his reign was diseased in his feet, until his disease was exceeding great: yet in his disease he sought not to the LORD, but to the physicians. And Asa slept with his fathers, and died in the one and fortieth year of his reign."*
>
> *2 Chr 16:12-14*

It is extremely important for us to trust God during our times of difficulty and need. Asa, the King of Judah brought glory to God and his nation but lost faith in his later years and began to trust the doctors more than he trusted God. As a result of this the disease that he acquired in the thirty-ninth year of his reign worsened until he died. The amazing thing is that a King that once prided himself in his obedience and loyalty to the Lord is now reduced to a weak and sickly person who seeks and depends on the doctors to restore him to health. The scripture gives this sad epithet to the story of this once shining star in the history of God's chosen people:

"yet in his disease he sought not to the Lord."

2 chr 16:12

King Asa didn't seek God for healing of his disease. Often times we say that we trust God but our actions prove something else. Anything that we trust more than Jesus will fail us. This is His plan for all of human kind. The word of God tells us in the fifth chapter of 1 Samuel that the Lord God knocked the Philistine deity Dagon over in his own temple cutting off his head and palms of his hands. In this same way Jesus will topple everything in our lives that we put our trust in. Dagon represents the things that we worship and trust in the place of Jesus.

"And when they arose early on the morrow morning, behold, Dagon was fallen upon his face to the ground before the ark of the LORD; and the head of Dagon and both the palms of his hands were cut off upon the threshold; only the stump of Dagon was left to him."

1 Sam 5:4 (KJV)

We can trust our physicians so much that we will not be able to hear the voice of our Father. As I searched the scriptures I attempted to find a word that would assure that God wants us to rely on men in our time of distress, but it could not be found. It appears that the Bible indicates the original and only purpose for physicians was in Egypt for the embalming of the dead. We have been taught that God gave doctors the ability and we should trust them because of their God given ability, but there are times that the doctor cannot help us. It is in these times that we must put our entire trust in the Lord God. We must turn from trusting man to trusting the living God. Jesus wants us to live that we might share His word and to release all that are hopeless and lost from their captivity that He might reveal His power in them.

" I shall not die, but live, and declare the works of the LORD."

Ps 118:17

In the old covenant God's people always trusted Him for their healing and Jesus declares healing as a benefit of being in covenant with him.

"Bless the LORD, O my soul, and forget not all his benefits: Who forgiveth all thine iniquities; who healeth all thy diseases;"

Ps 103:2-3

It is through our hopelessness that Jesus proves himself to us. If we do not come to the place of utter despair he cannot help us. It is all part of the process that God has ordained for us as we learn to live with and in Him. Jesus is crying out to us that His "grace is sufficient" and that He is our strength in weakness. Thank you Jesus!

"And he said unto me, My grace is sufficient for thee: for my strength is made perfect in weakness. Most gladly therefore will I rather glory in my infirmities, that the power of Christ may rest upon me. Therefore I take pleasure in infirmities, in reproaches, in necessities, in persecutions, in distresses for Christ's sake: for when I am weak, then am I strong."

2 Cor 12:9-10

The Living Bible says it like this

Each time he says: "No. But I am with you; that is all you need. My power shows up best in weak people." Now I am glad to boast about how weak I am; I am glad to be a living demonstration of Christ's power, instead of showing off my own power and abilities. Since I know it is all for Christ's good, I am quite happy about "the thorn," and about insults and hardships, persecutions and difficulties; for when I am weak, then I am strong-the less I have, the more I depend on him."

2 Cor 12:9-10 (TLB)

He expects us to believe Him.

When trouble enters our life, we exhaust all of our human efforts in our futile attempts to solve our own problems, and then we enter the place of utter hopelessness and despair, after which God helps us realize that He is the only source of our deliverance. It is at the end of this process that the Lord is glorified.

"But the God of all grace, who hath called us unto his eternal glory by Christ Jesus, after that ye have suffered a while, make you perfect, stablish, strengthen, settle you."

1 Peter 5:10

After we have suffered a while He will help us.

The journey to healing is less important than the finish line. Jesus is searching through the earth looking for someone that He can help when all hope is gone. Jesus is looking for an opportunity to show someone that He is God and that He cares about the things that concern His people. He's looking for someone that is ready to give up. He's looking for someone that recognizes their own frailty and weakness. He's looking for someone to heal. He's looking for you! At the end of all hope for any improvement in her condition the woman with the issue of blood pressed through a crowd and sneaks a touch of the Masters garment. When we are at our wits end and everything else has failed, when all hope is lost, sneak a touch. Now spend some time reflecting on this chapter and start your time of prayer with the following:

Dear Lord Jesus,

I have felt that all hope is lost and I need Your strength to make this journey and Your grace to make it to the finish line. Father, I love You, and I need to hear from You. I have been taught to trust in man all of my life and I cannot go on without the certainty that You are the Great Physician. I come to You now, broken and spent and have tried every other way to find relief. No one has been able to help me so I need You to prove that You are God. Prepare my heart now to experience your healing reality today and make me perfect. I love You in the name of Jesus. Amen

CHAPTER 4

MAKING HIS NAME GREAT

"When she had heard of Jesus, came in the press behind, and touched his garment. For she said, If I may touch but his clothes, I shall be whole."..Mark 5:27-28

OUR job in this earth is to make Jesus famous. The greatest name that has ever been uttered is Jesus. The name of Jesus is majestic, it is wonderful, and it is magnanimous, noble, worthy and all powerful. He entered this world as God in the flesh to free us from the bondages of sin and death.

"And the Word was made flesh, and dwelt among us, (and we beheld his glory, the glory as of the only begotten of the Father,) full of grace and truth."

John 1:14

"He that committeth sin is of the devil; for the devil sinneth from the beginning. For this purpose the Son of God was manifested, that he might destroy the works of the devil."

1 John 3:8

On top of that He allowed His creation to thrash and beat Him sealing our right to experience His healing power.

But he was wounded for our transgressions, he was bruised for our iniquities: the chastisement of our peace was upon him; and with his stripes we are healed.

Isa 53:5

We receive healing because of the beating that He took at Calvary. The Lord Jesus came to the attention of the multitudes because of the wondrous works that He performed. The blind received their sight, the lame walked, lepers were cleansed, the deaf could hear, and the dead were raised up. The report of His feats raced from one end of Judea to another and began to spill over the borders. No man had ever performed the miracles that Jesus did. God became a human being and walked among His people seeking opportunities to declare His power to man. His fame preceded Him to such an extent that John the Baptist sent word from prison questioning who He was. His incarceration in prison no doubt created some anxiety for John and he needed clarification from the master. In Jesus' reply to John's question we discover the manifestation of His purpose in the earth, to destroy the work of the devil. Only God can intervene in the affairs of men and change the course of history.

"The disciples of John the Baptist soon heard of all that Jesus was doing. When they told John about it, he sent two of his disciples to Jesus to ask him, Are you really the Messiah? Or shall we keep on looking for him? The two disciples found Jesus while he was curing many sick people of their various diseases-healing the lame and the blind and casting out evil spirits. When they asked him John's question, this was his reply: Go back to John and tell him all you have seen and heard here today: how those who were blind can see. The lame are walking without a limp. The lepers are completely healed. The deaf can hear again. The dead come back to life. And the poor are hearing the Good News. And tell him, Blessed is the one who does not lose his faith in me.

Luke 7:18-23 (TLB)

The name of Jesus is great and the only name available to bring us to salvation. The root meaning of Jesus is Jehovah, the self existent one has become our salvation. He is willing to save all those that call upon His name. In scripture names are very significant and represent the authority and ability of a person. During Luke's account in the book of Acts the declaration is made that the name of Jesus is the only name that can save us.

> *"Neither is there salvation in any other: for there is none other name under heaven given among men, whereby we must be saved."*
>
> *Acts 4:12*

The name of the Lord is a strong tower and provides help to the righteous who run into the name of Jesus. It is like a fortress or a hiding place that protects us from the troubles of this world.

> *"The name of the LORD is a strong tower: the righteous runneth into it, and is safe."*
>
> *Prov 18:10*

We assure our salvation and receive His power when we believe on His name. His name is the only way to eternal life and membership into His family.

> *"But as many as received him, to them gave He power to become the sons of God, even to them that believe on his name:"*
>
> *John 1:12*

If we believe in His name we will receive our miracle. Believing in His name requires becoming personally intimate with Him and obeying His word. Personal intimacy begins with seeking Him in prayer and devouring His word. In addition, fasting or abstaining from meals promotes a high level of intimacy and develops a breeding ground for miracles as we couple it with prayer and devotion to His word. Believing in His name seals the deal.

> *"Now when he was in Jerusalem at the passover, in the feast day, many believed in his name, when they saw the miracles which he did."*
> *John 2:23*

It is through faith in His name that we receive our healing. We must find our dependence in His name and totally rely on Him. It is like jumping out of an airplane without a parachute just because He said so. As we take the plunge we do it believing that we will not hit the ground because He has promised to rescue us from our deepest trouble.

> *"And His name through faith in His name hath made this man strong, whom ye see and know: yea, the faith which is by him hath given Him this perfect soundness in the presence of you all."*
> *Acts 3:16*

As we exemplify faith in His name it will cause Jesus to recognize our touch and heal our bodies. He knows us personally and will respond when He is touched by us. As you weep before the Lord, pray for the power of His name to be made real in your life. He will recognize the touch of faith.

> *Lord*
> *I trust in your name completely and believe if I call upon you I will be healed. Your name is the greatest sound that I have ever heard and I thank you for revealing yourself to me. Make your name real to me as I confess that the name of Jesus is the greatest name ever uttered. Help me to continue to make your name great as I share your faithfulness to every man and they see you in my life. Amen*

CHAPTER 5

WHO TOUCHED ME?

"Who touched me?" Jesus asked. Everyone denied it, and Peter said, "Master, so many are crowding against you...."

Luke 8:45

JESUS will recognize your touch. He knows us and can count every hair on our head. He's always there, watching over us and leading us to our purpose and destiny, but we must first realize our need to touch him. We have tried everything else and it has not been affective causing us to have additional torment, doubt, stress and hopelessness. It is amazing that we unequivocally follow the prescriptions of mere men and evade the prescription of God. Jesus is alive and is still divinely intervening in the affairs of humankind.

"Who touched me?" Jesus asked. Everyone denied it, and Peter said Master, so many are crowding against you.... " But Jesus told him, No, it was someone who deliberately touched me, for I felt healing power go out from me When the woman realized that Jesus knew, she began to tremble and fell to her knees before him and told why she had touched him and that now she was well. "Daughter," he said to her, your faith has healed you. Go in peace."

Luke 8:45-48 (TLB)

I NEED TO TOUCH HIM

"When she had heard of Jesus, came in the press behind, and touched his garment. For she said, If I may touch but his clothes, I shall be whole."

Mark 5: 27-28

When this woman with the issue of blood heard of Jesus she fought her way through the crowd for a opportunity to be healed of her pain. This woman had spent all her money on doctors and was not any better. This woman just like others before her received revelation of God's power in her indigence and sought after Him.

Jonah was in the belly of the big fish at the bottom of the ocean when he came to the realization of his utter depravity, and the prodigal son was eating dinner with the pigs at the revelation of his neediness for a move of God.

Then Jonah prayed unto the LORD his God out of the fish's belly, And said, I cried by reason of mine affliction unto the LORD, and he heard me; out of the belly of hell cried I, and thou heardest my voice.

Jonah 2:1-2

And when he came to himself, he said, How many hired servants of my father's have bread enough and to spare, and I perish with hunger!

Luke 15:17

The commonality between these two is that they came to themselves and acknowledged their absolute need and dependence on God. The woman with the issue of blood heard of Jesus and believed what she heard. Instead of pondering and questioning His ability to heal she believed and acted upon that belief. Suddenly, after hearing of Him her faith was activated and she began to press forward. It did not matter that the crowd was massive or that she was a woman or that she had an issue that made her unclean. She had taken the first step and now she needed to grasp hold of Him.

The first step is hearing. We need to hear of Him.

"So then faith cometh by hearing, and hearing by the word of God"
Rom 10:17

The second step is to believe what we hear.

"You can never please God without faith, without depending on him. Anyone who wants to come to God must believe that there is a God and that he rewards those who sincerely look for him"
Heb 11:6. (TLB)

The third step is to take action.

Faith is a verb and requires action on the part of the one that believes. What action do you need to take? Get out a pen and paper and write three action steps you will take that prove you believe the word of God. In the midst of all her years of anguish she acted on what she believed and took a leap of faith saying within herself "If I could but touch the hem of His garment". Where are you? Are you at the end of your rope? Have you given up hope? Our hopelessness is the greatest opportunity for Jesus to give us a miracle and turn our situation around. He loves to confound the wisdom of men by performing the impossible.

A TOUCH OF FAITH

With a crowd pressing against Him, Jesus could feel that one touch of faith. Someone believed that He was a healer with all power and reached for Him. This woman set aside all the odds against her and pressed through a massive crowd in order to release her faith. As her faith touched him, Jesus felt healing flow out of His body.

Those that were with Him couldn't understand how He felt one touch in such a great crowd but Jesus perceived that one deliberate touch. It was a purposed touch that elicited a response from the King. He said someone touched me on purpose and I felt it. There is a flow that will proceed forth from God with the right touch. There are healing oils that flow from the throne of God with the right touch. There is a touch that He can feel. There is a touch that will heal us. There is a touch that will change us in one instant. You might be saying, but how can I touch Him? He seems so far away. My health is failing. My situation is hopeless. Consider now the word of God. Take a small step of faith. Start with some mustard seed faith and ask God to heal you.

"And all things, whatsoever ye shall ask in prayer, believing, ye shall receive."

Matt 21:22

"Ask, and it shall be given you; seek, and ye shall find; knock, and it shall be opened unto you:"

Matt 7:7

SNEAK A TOUCH

This woman was at the end of the rope without any hope that there would be any improvement in her condition but something breaks inside of her and she presses through a crowd and sneaks a touch of the

Masters garment. Sneaking a touch does not mean that we have to be sneaky, but it means that we have to deviate from our present course and become determined to reach and receive an answer from the Lord. We must say inside of ourselves "I won't let You go until you bless me." There is a steadfastness that we must obtain in times of trouble where we develop a total reliance upon Jesus. We must stop treating Him like a fictional character but as a Great and Mighty Father. Do not give up and do not let go. **Sneak a touch!** Jesus loves it when we interrupt Him on His way somewhere else. When Lazarus died, Jesus stayed where He was for two days knowing that He was going to raise Lazarus from the dead. Remember, Jesus already knows the date and time of your deliverance, so sneak a touch. As we touch Him, He recognizes our need. He is not looking for us in order to heal us. He is looking for us to touch Him for our healing.

"When he had heard therefore that he was sick, he abode two days still in the same place where he was."

John 11:6

When we are at our wits end and everything else has failed, sneak a touch. This woman stopped to touch Him and she was immediately healed. There is a touch that the master will feel. This touch is felt through our suffering and tears. We must decide that only He can help us and expect Him to do exactly that. Right where you are, on your bed, in your car, in your office began to sneak a touch. Our situation requires a falling down, just like the women with the issue of blood, a falling down at his feet, exposing where we are, and worshipping Him. Hey, we've tried everything else. What can it hurt! We've got to use desperate measures for desperate times. Who is it that's in need of a touch? Is it you? Is it a loved one? A husband? A wife? A Child? Let's press through the crowd and touch Him. Sometimes the crowd may not be a throng of people. Maybe it's the perceived reality of a doctor's report, or the negative words that have been spoken. Perhaps you've been told that your situation is hopeless and you don't have much time. Perhaps you can't see a visible change and the symptoms are getting worse. Are these words crowding out your Faith and hindering you from believing that Jesus loves and cares for you?

In the instant that the women touched Him the twelve-year flow of blood stopped and she was immediately healed. There is a touch that the master will feel. It involves a pure heart and an earnest expectation from us.

Find a place to lie out and cry before God and pray. Just talk to Him and tell Him what you feel. Tell Him about you fears and your hopes. Love on Him and listen for His voice. Take a few moments, shut out the crowd pray this prayer and spend time asking the Father to increase your faith and prepare your heart to touch Him. Your faith will make you whole.

Dear Heavenly Father,

I come to you today asking for the wisdom to touch you. I know that my heart has not always been true toward you and I have trusted in others more than I have trusted in you. Please prepare my heart to touch you. I am desperate to touch the hem of your garment and be made whole and free. I love you so much. In my own way I have come to sneak a touch today. Hear me Lord and answer me. I have not always trusted you like I should, but today I choose to change my ways. Forgive me for all the years that I disregarded your commands and your voice and allow me to have a new start. I touch you, I touch you, and I touch you and I touch you, Lord. Amen

CHAPTER 6

YOUR FAITH HAS MADE YOU WHOLE

"Then He touched their eyes, According to your faith be it unto you"

Matt 9:29

GOD wants us to trust in Him for everything. We have made the gospel hard. The message to be conveyed by us is that it is not by power or by might, but by the power of God that we are made whole. The scriptures declare all things are possible to those that believe. We take many chances in life so let's take a chance on our heavenly Father. Oftentimes we can believe for others but when it comes to believing for our own situations we begin to doubt. God doesn't want us to doubt. He wants us to believe in Him. The Lord says if we believe without doubting we shall receive what we are asking for. Paul said he fought a good fight and finished his course. Believing God is a fight that will take all of our strength to win but as we continue to hold on to faith we will win.

"I have fought a good fight, I have finished my course, I have kept the faith:"

2 Tim 4:7

The Apostle Paul fought a good fight. He held on to God in spite of the circumstances he faced in life. He had a testimony that would have caused most men to shrink back. Paul was on a mission and he knew what his purpose was. He had an assignment from God and no matter what; he was going to finish it. He learned how to believe God for the impossible with courage and joy.

> *"Wherefore, sirs, be of good cheer: for I believe God, that it shall be even as it was told me"*
>
> *Acts 27:25*

> *"So take courage! For I believe God! It will be just as he said!"*
>
> *Acts 27:25 (TLB)*

Faith is a condition that we cannot live without. Faith grounds us to God's promises. We need to be constantly sure of His promises for us to maintain our footing. It's like walking on slippery rocks, if you're not steadfast and alert you could lose your footing and fall. We must nurture the faith that God has given us by constantly bathing it in prayer, worship and His word because it pleases Him when we believe in Him. If we are void of faith it is impossible for us to be fully accepted by Him.

> *"But without faith it is impossible to please him: for he that cometh to God must believe that he is, and that he is a rewarder of them that diligently seek him."*
>
> *Heb 11:6*

The Living Bible expresses clearly, that we can never please God if we don't trust Him.

> *"You can never please God without faith, without depending on him. Anyone who wants to come to God must believe that there is a God and that he rewards those who sincerely look for him."*
>
> *Heb 11:6 (TLB)*

We must depend on Him. We cannot make it without Him. He is our hope and our confidence. The scriptures are not just words, but they are keys that will unlock the mysteries of God.

"Commit thy way unto the LORD; trust also in him; and he shall bring it to pass."

Ps 37:5

When the scripture say commit thy way unto the Lord it gives us the sense of wallowing in Him or rolling together with Him as one. In other words my life must become His life. The two must become one flesh. I must be in Him, and He in me.

'I have been crucified with Christ: and I myself no longer live, but Christ lives in me."

Gal 2:20 (TLB)

'Jesus answered and said unto them, Verily I say unto you, If ye have faith, and doubt not, ye shall not only do this which is done to the fig tree, but also if ye shall say unto this mountain, Be thou removed, and be thou cast into the sea; it shall be done. And all things, whatsoever ye shall ask in prayer, believing, ye shall receive."

Matt 21:21-22

Life is not always easy so it is important that we believe God to find relief. We must remember that it is God that spoke and the world came into existence. He healed the sick, cast out devils, caused the elements to obey Him, and raised the dead. We need to align ourselves to the only One that can do the impossible. Our faith is exemplified when we can stand against all odds and believe that Jesus will do exactly what He said that He would do.

I recall a time shortly after I received the Holy Ghost and I was faced with a physical challenge. I had been having excruciating pain in my lower abdomen for months and finally decided to go to the doctor. The doctor shared his prognosis with me and explained his plan for treatment. He told me that I had acute endometriosis and would need a partial or complete hysterectomy along with an aggressive treatment that would cause me to lose hair, gain weight, possible acne, and other side effects. As I left the doctor's office, I walked into the parking lot, lifted my hands and declared, "Lord you're going to have to heal me because I'm not going to let this man touch me." I was healed instantly and never had another problem with endometriosis. Had I trusted in the doctors word I would have had a hysterectomy and not given birth to my four youngest children. Our faith is not great but the faith of God in us is great.

When we make the decision to believe that only Jesus can help us and refuse the intervention of men, the faith of God for healing is activated in our life. I realized at that point in my life that the doctors were only human and there is limit to what they can do. It is God's faith and healing power that makes us whole. As we reflect on that woman with the issue of blood we recall that one of the key elements of her hopelessness was trusting in man without obtaining any relief for her pain. As Jesus became her reality the faith of God swelled within her and she was instantly healed of her infirmity.

As Paul was preaching he observed a lame man listening intently to his message and perceived that he had faith to be healed. He simply told him to get up and walk and this man stood up walking.

While they were at Lystra, they came upon a man with crippled feet who had been that way from birth, so he had never walked. He was listening as Paul preached, and Paul noticed him and realized he had faith to be healed. So Paul called to him, "Stand up!" and the man leaped to his feet and started walking!

Acts 14:8-10 (TLB)

There is a similar account of blind men that followed Jesus and received their healing.

> *And when he was come into the house, the blind men came to him: and Jesus saith unto them, Believe ye that I am able to do this? They said unto him, Yea, Lord. Then touched he their eyes, saying, According to your faith be it unto you.*
>
> *Matt 9:28-29*

Jesus asked the blind men if they believed it was possible to be healed and they answered yes. As he touched their eyes Jesus made a statement that presented the key to His healing flow, "according to your faith". We receive healing according to our faith in His ability to do it. Even though we desire to have faith and believe God the day will come when our faith will be tried. It is during these times that we must fight to hold on to the word of the Lord. Take a few moments and pray for God to increase your faith.

THE TRYING OF OUR FAITH

In James chapter one and verse three he tells us that our faith will be tried:

> *"Knowing this, that the trying of your faith worketh patience." James 1:3*

When James spoke of the trying of our faith he knew that we would be tested in the very thing that we said we believed God for. Testing proves our trustworthiness to God and allows us to see what our response will be under fire. Our trials also help us to acquire patience which will cause us to be strong in God as we obtain greater character and wisdom. We used a saying as children; "talk is cheap" or "put your money where your mouth is". In order for us to put our money where our mouth is, we must walk through the trying of our faith. When I received the doctor's report that I had cancer I immediately began to walk in fear. I cried for two days and wondered if God was going to heal me. After all, I had given my whole life to Him and had never looked back. It didn't help that I hadn't heard a word from Him during the first two weeks. I was depressed and I wondered if I would die, and have to leave my husband and children. Even though I continued to seek God I couldn't seem to obtain the victory over my thought life but I continued to confess the word of the Lord and believe Him. Finally, one morning in prayer I heard the Lord say, "You shall live and not die".

> *"for when the way is rough, your patience has a chance to grow. So let it grow, and don't try to squirm out of your problems. For when your patience is finally in full bloom, then you will be ready for anything, strong in character, full and complete."*
>
> *James 1:3-7*

Many of the trials that we face are designed to develop patience in us. Patience at its greatest point will strengthen our character and gives us a sense of completion. The circumstances of life that we are called to go through are not always easy, but Jesus is trying to make us perfect, just like He is perfect. Through my ordeal I learned that by trusting God I will reap great rewards even in a lengthy trial. My desire is to trust Him with all my heart, mind, body and soul.

> *"We can rejoice, too, when we run into problems and trials, for we know that they help us develop endurance. And endurance develops strength of character, and character strengthens our confident hope of salvation. And this hope will not lead to disappointment. For we*

know how dearly God loves us, because he has given us the Holy Spirit
to fill our hearts with his love"

Rom 5:3-7

When all hope is lost we need faith. Faith is an attitude of believing God It is a strong opinion about the truth of His word. As we look back over the words of the Apostle Paul it is noteworthy that he talked about obtaining the victory over deterrents to his faith and used the analogy of fighting. We are in the fight of our life and Jesus is fighting with us. Paul said to Timothy

'I have fought a good fight, I have finished my course, I have kept the faith:"

2 Tim 4:7

When all hope is lost we must embark upon the course that God has established for us and remember that He will stand with us in any fight we have. He will never let us fight unless He speaks to us first. God will tell His prophets where you are going next.

Lord Jesus,
I can feel Your faith swelling within and I thank you for your promise to heal me. Please don't let me waiver when you try me, because I want you to be pleased with me as you heal me according to the faith that you have given to me. I realize that I have been weak but I feel a new strength rising within me. Please give me the grace to stand with your faith so that the world will know that you are God. Please increase my faith. Thank you for being my healer.

CHAPTER 7

GOD WILL TELL HIS PROPHETS FIRST

"Surely the Lord GOD will do nothing, but he revealeth his secret unto his servants the prophets."

Amos 3:7

GOD will always give us a word concerning our circumstances to prepare us for what is to come. March 2005, the doctor's office called for me to come in. I was out of town with my son's basketball team and had just returned. They asked if I could come for an appointment in 30 minutes. My husband was at the gym so I went alone to meet the doctors. On the way to the appointment God spoke to me and said, "Tell them to make up their mind what they will do before they get the word." I felt that God was giving me a message for the people of God. Make up your mind before trouble comes. Plot your course beforehand to help eliminate fear on your journey. We must trust God for His positive results before we begin the process.

As I approached the doctor's office I remembered what God had told me almost twenty years prior. My husband and I had begun our ministry and were new pastors in the city of Sunnyvale, California. The spirit of the Lord was so powerful in our services that we regularly experienced manifestations of healing and deliverance. One Sunday night during our evening worship services God spoke to me. A young woman, who had recently come to Jesus, walked to the back of the church where I was sitting. I will never forget her. Her name was Christy. She fell into my lap weeping and said, "God told me that He was going to heal you of cancer in your left breast." I was so startled by this and could not get it out of my mind because this was so unlike her. I knew immediately that it was God speaking through her. I couldn't rebuke it or deny it because it was Him. As the years went by I would always remember the word and wondered if it would come to pass. I never told anyone about what was spoken that night, not even my husband. You don't ever want to speak something like this for fear that it might give life to the words. Secretly, we say within ourselves, oh no God, not that. But when God has spoken a thing it will surly come to pass. When I discovered the lump, I knew that it was cancer.

The week prior to having the biopsy I confided in a few people that I knew would pray and started to seek God. Everyone that I confided in had a word of encouragement for me and unilaterally proclaimed that I would receive a good report from the doctors. I could not hear the Lord say anything concerning the biopsy and continued to remember what Christy said all those years ago, "God said He was going to heal you of cancer in your left breast."

When people love you they automatically want the best for you. That is why we get so disappointed when we proclaim that a thing is God and it does not come to pass. We must continually listen for the voice of our Father. He proclaims the truth and we will never fully understand the truth until we seek Him for it. I held on to my faith by remembering all of the miracles that I had witnessed over the years.

God will not allow the great tragedies of your life to come until He has prepared you and is sure that you are ready. Our Lord is not waiting for us to mess up and fall. He is cheering us on reaffirming that we can make it through any obstacle course that He sets up in our life.

A Friend Dies

What happened to my friend changed my life. One of my very best friends died of cancer. We grew up together and were so close in high school that we were inseparable. It wasn't until I went away to the University of Nebraska that our relationship grew distant. As the years passed we talked less and less but my love for her friendship was always constant. She married and started her family in another city and I moved to California. When I heard that she had breast cancer and was not expected to live I got on a plane and went to be with her. We were new pastors and I believed with all my heart that God would heal her because of my prayers. I don't know why God heals some and not others but I learned a valuable lesson during the last week that I spent with her. I cannot give another man total control over my life. Doctors are talented and skilled individuals and have helped many sick regain their strength and health, but there are certain conditions in which the doctor cannot change the prognosis because only Jesus can heal the incurable. For me cancer was that condition. There is no cure for cancer. Modern technology and medical science can slow the process in some people but only God can permanently remove the condition.

The moment that changed my life was the day that my friend died. Everyone that loved her stood around her bedside praying and weeping as she took her last breath. When she was gone I heard someone say with extreme anguish, "she went through all of this and she still died." You see she went through all the traditional cancer treatments; chemotherapy, radiation, mastectomy and death. I loved her so much and wanted her to live but she didn't. I began to realize on that day that the doctors can't always help and I made up my mind that I would trust Jesus. That's what Jesus did, He died to save many. Through the death of my friend many will live. After this I began to seek God for the secret of His healing flow.

THE ROAD LESS TRAVELED

There is nothing like the words "It's Cancer." When I walked into the doctor's office I felt strange, excited and dreadful all at the same time. I was excited that God had chosen me but felt a sense of dread at the same time because I wasn't sure I could go through the test. When I walked in, the doctor barely looked at me and asked if he could examine the scar from the biopsy. I wondered in myself what his lack of eye contact meant. The next words that he spoke caused me to hold my breath for a moment. He spoke in an extremely cold manner with what appeared to be a smirk on his face, "well, the bad news is its cancer". I sat there wondering; well what's the good news. Next, he began to recite my treatment options. First, he recommended that we remove the breast. Secondly, we could choose to perform a lumpectomy, which would involve excising a larger area around the lump, and removing the lymph nodes for testing. This would be followed by radiation treatment and chemotherapy. I couldn't grasp the magnitude of his recommendation since I had only been in the hospital for sickness once in my entire life. What does this mean I thought? Where is the good news? Lord I need to hear from you.

The Lord is amazing! When trouble comes into our lives He truly walks us through the process. Without any hesitation I opened my mouth and began to speak. I said "Doc, you will have to bear with me, because I probably will not let you treat me. You see, I am a strong believer in Jesus and almost twenty years ago someone told me that God was going to heal me of cancer in my left breast and here it is." He offered me informational booklets on breast cancer which I refused because I thought they would cause me to fear and succumb to the intensity of the situation. I needed to hear a strong word from my Father. I had to take the road less traveled.

I left the doctor's office and went immediately home. I needed to talk to my husband and I needed to talk to Jesus. God has displayed His miraculous healing power in his life also. When I pulled up to the house he was in the car in front of the house, and I believe that this was the first in a series of miracles that would lead me to reject the opinions of man and believe Jesus. My daughters were waiting for me inside the house and I didn't want to tell them before I could come to grips with what had just happened. I jumped in the car with him and said "drive". He was concerned and asked me what was wrong. I said "the doctor said its cancer." He said "no way" and I said "yes way", and then there was silence. God speaks to us in many ways but I will never forget how He spoke on that day.

As we were driving up the street we came to a billboard on the side of the road that totally amazed me and caused faith to leap within me. Right there on the side of the road, not five minutes from home there was a billboard and it said, *"LAST YEAR CANCER, THIS YEAR TUSCANY, MIRACLES HAPPEN."* I made up my mind that I would not do anything unless I had total direction from God. There are promises that God made that will truly come to pass in your life. Each one of us will have an experience in the darkness but there will also be a Tuscan experience if we believe Jesus. I get chocked up every time I think about that billboard and begin to worship my God for His faithfulness to me. God is faithful and He will not allow you to be ashamed when you trust Him. Let's stop here to worship and thank the Lord for all of His faithfulness to us. Lord, I believe that I will trust you. I am going to Tuscany.

Lord Jesus
I worship you today for all of your faithfulness to me. My heart is filled
with love and joy because of what you have done in my life. I trust you
with all of my heart, soul and strength and am so thankful that you called

me to know You. Lord break through my darkness and give me a Tuscan experience. Lord I love you and I worship your holy name. Amen

Chapter 8

Last Year Cancer, This Year Tuscany

'For the thing which I greatly feared is come upon me, and that which I was afraid of is come unto me."

Job 3:25

I believe that my life was changed when I saw that Tuscany billboard. I could not believe that I saw the words correctly; "Last Year Cancer, this Year Tuscany, Miracles happen". I didn't even know where Tuscany was. I had never been to Europe and had no intention of ever going. I did know that my Father was talking to me and had temporarily dried my ears and took away my fear. I knew two things for certain; God was with me and I was going to Tuscany. The following year in September, I went to Tuscany. My husband and I flew to Italy and stayed in a breathtaking villa in the Tuscan countryside not far from Florence. We traveled by train to various parts of Italy including Florence, Rome and Venice. I was completely in awe of the beauty that God has created in this earth. Rome was my favorite spot because it was amazing and rich with history and I felt close to the suffering that are forefathers in the gospel experienced in that city. As we passed the Coliseum for the first time I began to weep as I remembered accounts of the suffering and murder of God's people at the hands of the Roman Emperors. We prayed and interceded at the Vatican for the people of the world asking the Lord to remove the scales from their eyes that they might know him, and we rebuked the spirit of religion. It is religion and its religious systems that keep us in a place where we cannot find God. We will always remember what the Lord has done for us when we think of Tuscany. One good thing that cancer did for me was to cause me to enlarge the borders of my tent and go where I had never gone before. If it had not been for the message from Jesus, I would probably have never gone to this beautiful area of the world. I am sharing this with you because I need to encourage you to hold on to faith in God. It is not over until He says so.

Remember, God will always give signs to His children. When we believe Him, He obligates Himself to make His word true. Nothing will ever take us by surprise when we walk with Jesus. I have been blessed with a wonderful life. I have a husband that I adore and who loves me unconditionally and we have nine wonderful children, who God has given us promises concerning:

"But the seed of the righteous shall be delivered"

Prove 11:21

They have given us more joy than sorrow and have filled our life with so much love and happiness. God has also blessed us with a two more beautiful daughters through marriage to our sons, 10 wonderful grandchildren, a phenomenal congregation and so many other family and friends that love us. I have always felt extremely blessed and grateful to God for the life that He has given me and I am sure that you have been blessed also

The Lord sets up our life and causes circumstances to come in order to accomplish His will. You see we all have a journey that we must take and we will never be totally effective until we walk through the proof of our ministry.

"But watch thou in all things, endure afflictions, do the work of an evangelist, make full proof of thy ministry."

2 Tim 4:5

Job also says,

"I was not in safety, neither had I rest, neither was I quiet; yet trouble came."

Job 3:26

Trouble usually comes when we least expect it. Just like Job, I was serving God the best that I could and walking in obedience to His word, but trouble still came. I have learned so much through the experiences that God has chosen for my life. I can never be good enough or obedient enough to divert my assigned test and trials or keep them from happening. In order to have God's strength, I must have my weakness. I must become helpless and hopeless in myself while being strengthened in the power of His might. One of life's greatest questions is why. Why am I going through this? Why doesn't God help me? Why won't this end?

"Why is a man allowed to be born if God is only going to give him a hopeless life of uselessness and frustration? I cannot eat for sighing; my groans pour out like water. What I always feared has happened to me. I was not fat and lazy, yet trouble struck me down."

Job 3:23-4:1 (TLB)

Job said that the thing he feared the most had come upon him. He speaks for all of us because deep inside there is the fear of something happening to us that we run from and secretly tremble when we think about it. Inevitably, it will come because we must walk in perfect love and fear works against perfect love. I made up my mind a long time ago that I had to trust Jesus with my entire life, soul and being. As much as

I tried I couldn't muster up the kind of faith needed to walk in this life without fear and have lived by the principle that I serve him out of fear. I am not afraid of His judgments but I am afraid of being away from Him and not having His help when trouble comes. Because of this I continue to pray, fast, praise Him and worship. Your labor is not in vain and you will receive your reward.

There is always something new to fear and we will always have new challenges. I had many fears in my life that I prayed for God to remove from me. The crazy thing is that in order for the fear to move we must face the fear. God is so great that He begins the preparation for the test long before it is manifested in your life. He also walks through the fire with us and gives us His faith to continue to the end. It is His faith that helped me, because my faith is human but His faith is supernatural. Our faith will leave us stagnant but His faith will move us to the front of the line. Halleluiah!

Lord Jesus,

Thank you for faith to believe. I need a Tuscan experience and I am asking you to bring it to pass. My heart is full and I am so grateful to you for your help and amazing kindness to me. I don't want to be in this world without you and am asking you to take me to the front of the line. I love you with all of my heart. Amen

CHAPTER 9

THE FRONT OF THE LINE

"Beloved, think it not strange concerning the fiery trial which is to try you, as though some strange thing happened to You."

I Pe 4:12

JUST before I was diagnosed I heard the Lord say to me "I am taking you to the front of the line". Naturally, I thought that He meant I was about to come out of obscurity and do great things for Him. Little did I realize that God's front of the line meant that I was on His schedule for testing. It seems like I had been in the fiery furnace since the day I received Jesus Christ. There was a time that I asked Him when my tests and trials would end and He said "When I come." We cannot eliminate our times of testing for any reason. It does not matter if we are good and follow the letter and spirit of His word without error. God established our destiny before the foundation of the earth to fulfill His purpose. We can never reach our pre-destined purpose in life if we continue to avoid the circumstances that frighten us. Secretly, we all want to do the will of God with excellence. I have always had a desire to leave my mark on this world and to become great in God, but greatness always comes with a price. We have to pay a great price to stand in the front of the line. The front line is the first place of defense and the first place of attack. I am excited about the front of the line because it is there that you can receive your miracle. The women with the issue of blood pressed her way to the front of the line and would not be held back from receiving what the Master alone could give her. She was desperate for her healing as we must become desperate. Jesus does not want us to be fearful. Fear is not an attribute of God. At times we forget who Jesus is and the power that He possesses. At our time appointed to take the seat at the front of the line we must remember that Jesus is with us. He has promised never to leave us or forsake us. This generation must learn to totally trust and depend upon the Lord.

We have a great example from the Lord Himself when He took his place at the front of the line. The night that Jesus went to the garden at Gethsemane to pray He took his disciples with Him to give us a great object lesson. We must keep prayer in the fore front of our lives. If we do not have a consistent and focused prayer life we will not have power in our time of need.

"And they came to a place which was named Gethsemane: and he saith to his disciples, Sit ye here, while I shall pray."

Mark 14:32

The very meaning of Gethsemane depicts a sense of powerless and suffering. The meaning of the word Gethsemane is derived from a word of Aramaic origin that denotes a crushing or squeezing similar to grapes in a wine press. The essence of the fruit will never be obtained until it is pressed and crushed. It was at Gethsemane that our Lord struggled with the path to His destiny and questioned His course. When we face uncertainty in our life it is possible to be overtaken with sorrow Because Jesus was our perfect example He was not exempt from pain and sorrow.

"And saith unto them, My soul is exceeding sorrowful unto death: tarry ye here, and watch"

Mark 14:34

In many ways it becomes the story of our life. We know that there is a road ahead of us that may be uncomfortable and we would rather not take the trip. Jesus asked if it were possible to have the cup of His affliction removed. We don't want to go through sickness and disease, struggles or worry but the time will come that we will all keep the appointment. We have an appointment for suffering but we also have an appointment for healing.

In the the third chapter of the book of Acts there was a man sitting in front of the Gate Beautiful begging alms from those that passed by. The providence of God had Peter and John walking to church for prayer at the exact moment that Jesus had appointed for this man's miracle. He was carried to the gate on a daily basis and his time of appointment had finally come. Peter and John fastened their eyes on him and declared their lack of monetary wealth but emphasized the greatness of the power of God in them to heal this poor man. They said that they didn't have money but they did have his healing and caused the man to walk for the first time in his life. It is ironic that the original Greek meaning for the word beautiful is "belonging to the right time or season, in other words God has a time or season set for our healing." The Lord is telling us that there is a time and a season for us to experience freedom from sickness and disease.

And a certain man lame from his mother's womb was carried, whom they laid daily at the gate of the temple which is called Beautiful, to ask alms of them that entered into the temple; Who seeing Peter and John about to go into the temple asked an alms. And Peter, fastening his eyes upon him with John, said, Look on us. And he gave heed unto them, expecting to receive something of them. Then Peter said, Silver and gold have I none; but such as I have give I thee: In the name of Jesus Christ of Nazareth rise up and walk. And he took him by the right hand, and lifted him up: and immediately his feet and ancle bones received strength. And he leaping up stood, and walked, and entered with them into the temple, walking, and leaping, and praising God. And all the people saw him walking and praising God Acts 3:2-9 :

Jesus knew what course was ahead of Him but He went to the cross in spite of the hard trial, in order to become an example when our time arrives for a front of the line experience.

"And he went forward a little, and fell on the ground, and prayed that, if it were possible, the hour might pass from him. And he said, Abba, Father, all things are possible unto thee; take away this cup from me: nevertheless not what I will, but what thou wilt."

Mark 14:35-36

Jesus understands how we feel and why it is so easy for us to put ourselves in the hands of men instead of leaning and depending upon Him. Our greatest and most profound instruction will take place at the front of the line. It is here that we will learn to enter into the gate of faith where fear is absent. Even though we experience pain and sorrow in our affliction we do not have to remain in the press. Jesus is waiting for the production of our final product. He wants the sweetness of the essence to flow from our being just like it did from His. Even in our present distress we are learning and growing and God has an expected end for us. He wants to heal us but we cannot serve two masters. Our Father is telling us to embrace the front of the line, trust Him and defeat fear. We may not understand the path that we are on but if we trust Him on it we will receive a miracle. He promised and He cannot lie. The Bible says:

God is not a man, that he should lie; neither the son of man, that he should repent: hath he said, and shall he not do it? or hath he spoken, and shall he not make it good?

Num 23:19

"Trust in the LORD with all thine heart; and lean not unto thine own understanding. In all thy ways acknowledge him, and he shall direct thy paths"

Prov 3:5-6

"This High Priest of ours understands our weaknesses since he had the same temptations we do, though he never once gave way to them and sinned."

Heb 4:14-15 (TLB)

Take a moment right now and begin to press your way to the front of the line. Yes, you can do it right now. Find a secluded private place, fall on your knees and cry out to God, "Heal me Lord". If you can't move from where you are cry out anyway. Begin to talk to him and pour out your heart to him. I promise you that He understands and will allow you to see Him face to face.

Father,
Thank you for taking me to the front of the line. Now I realize that it is not a negative experience even though my time here is painful. I understand that you made this appointment for me and my season is here. Help me to stand in line and finish my course knowing that you cannot lie and will keep every promise from your word. I thank you for the courage and faith to stand. Thank you Jesus. Halleluiah Amen

Chapter 10

Face to Face

"And Jacob called the name of the place Peniel: for I have seen God face to face, and my life is preserved."

Gen 32:30

THE key to long life and healing is found in the face of the Lord. Seeking His face will render significant results. Much can be learned from the experiences of Jacob and Jeroboam's encounter with the Lord. Each man was at a turning point in his life when God intervened in time and space to give them a miracle. Seeing God face to face is the call of our day. We have tried everything else and it has all failed us. We go through our entire life much like the man that waited at the pool of Bethesda. Bethesda, which means the house of grace, was the site of a pool with five porches where invalids set and waited for their turn to enter the water which was believed to have healing virtue. Throngs of infirmed people would lay at the pool waiting their turn, much like a hospital waiting room.

"After this there was a feast of the Jews; and Jesus went up to Jerusalem. Now there is at Jerusalem by the sheep market a pool, which is called in the Hebrew tongue Bethesda, having five porches. In these lay a great multitude of impotent folk, of blind, halt, withered, waiting for the moving of the water. For an angel went down at a certain season into the pool, and troubled the water: whosoever then first after

the troubling of the water stepped in was made whole of whatsoever
disease he had. And a certain man was there, which had an infirmity
thirty and eight years. When Jesus saw him lie, and knew that he had
been now a long time in that case, he saith unto him, Wilt thou be
made whole?"

John 5:1-6

It is amazing when we consider the scene at that pool. Hundreds, possibly thousands, of sick and debilitated people were waiting for the assistance of a mere man when the God of the universe was with them. Jesus was walking with them and they didn't even recognize it. The same is true today. We put all of our hopes for recovery in man when Jesus is the only one who can mend and heal us.

WILT THOU BE MADE WHOLE?

The most profound question ever asked is, "wilt though be made whole"? Jesus has the ability to heal us but He needs us to acknowledge our need for Him to do it. Jesus' reputation preceded Him because of all the miracles that He had done, but the lame man was still looking for human help. There will come a point in time when humanity cannot help us. At this point we need the supernatural help of God. Suddenly after thirty-eight years with his condition this man saw the light, said yes to Jesus and was miraculously healed. We need a face to face encounter with the Lord Jesus Christ.

In another moment of desperation Jacob held on to God for an entire night and had his life completely changed. We will spend hours, days, weeks, months and years in the offices of physicians but we will not spend one night with God in prayer. One night of conversation with Him will change the course of your entire life.

"And Jacob was left alone; and there wrestled a man with him until the breaking of the day."

Gen 32:24

FACE TO FACE

God wants us to get so close to Him that we can see His face and feel His breath. Each painful demarcation in the life of the godly is marked by the voice of God speaking to us out of obscurity. When I saw Him and He blew the wind of His breathe into me I was healed. Many years prior the Lord gave me the breathe of His spirit when He filled me with the Holy Ghost. There is always evidence when we have an up close and personal encounter with Jesus. The release of His benefits in our midst is proof positive that we have been with him. Intimacy with the Lord will always result in the release of His healing flow of benefits.

Jacob attributed the saving of his life to a personal encounter with God and marked this face to face meeting by calling that place Peniel, meaning the house of God.

"And Jacob called the name of the place Peniel: for I have seen God face to face, and my life is preserved."

Gen 32:30

Jeroboam, king of Israel realized the importance of seeing the face of God He entreated the prophet to seek God's face to heal his hand that was withered as a result of the chastisement of the Lord. The scripture simply states that the man of God sought the face of God and the king's hand was healed. The Lord wants you to seek His face. He isn't hiding from you. He is waiting for you to come to Him for help.

"And the king answered and said unto the man of God, Intreat now the face of the LORD thy God, and pray for me, that my hand may be

restored me again. And the man of God besought the LORD, and the king's hand was restored him again, and became as it was before."

1 Kings 13:6

"Let us therefore come boldly unto the throne of grace, that we may obtain mercy, and find grace to help in time of need."

Heb 4:16

There is a people in this earth that have the same desire to see Him. We long for Him. Our hearts pant after Him.

"As the hart panteth after the water brooks, so panteth my soul after thee, O God."

Psalms 42:1

After my cancer diagnosis, I spent three months in prayer seeking the face of God for direction. During these three months I refused to return to the doctor and refused all treatment. I needed to find the Lord and look into His face to receive my instructions from him. The hardest part of the whole ordeal was sharing with my children about the cancer. There were many tears that flowed in those three months but we made it through. The doctor's office called me several times to get me back into the office for treatment, but God helped me to stay strong. Twice I agreed to come in when fear attacked me, but I totally forgot when the appointment time came. One morning while I was in my closet praying, I heard the Lord say; "You shall live and not die". I wondered if the voice I heard that morning was really God or me, and ignored it while continuing in prayer.

THE BREATH OF GOD

Three months after the initial diagnosis I received that strong word from God that I had been searching for. While I was asleep, the Lord Jesus Christ entered my dreams and spoke directly to me. I saw Him that night and my life was changed forever. In my dream, He glared at me with eyes of fire as I marveled at His presence. He was of a tall stature but I could only concentrate on His eyes. The eyes captured me and began to draw me into His presence. The most memorable thing about this encounter was the way He looked at me and what He said. He lifted both of His hands, smiled broadly like a proud father and said with a broadest smile and a chuckle "CRAaaaaaZY". At that moment, I realized that His words seemed to be the exact opposite of the doctors' voice at the time of diagnosis. I now realize that anyone that will stand in faith and truly believe God, will be looked upon as crazy. John the Baptist was crazy, Elijah was crazy, Paul was crazy and I am crazy. Thank you Jesus! At any rate, He grabbed me, and began to pull me toward Him. At first, I thought an unfamiliar man was trying to kiss me, so I screeched EEHEW. But when I realized it was the Lord I felt a great rush of expectation as I waited in awe of Him. As He placed His face onto mine, His face began to melt like hot wax onto my face. Then the most amazing thing happened, He opened His mouth and blew a great wind into my belly. I experienced the awesome breath of God. As I felt the wind fill my belly I experienced a sensation of floating and immediately awoke with exhilarating joy. Jesus actually came into my dream and healed me. I knew that I was healed and worshipped Him for giving me such a strong word.

The next morning I called the doctor to make an appointment to receive the proof that I was healed. When I arrived at his office, I began to tell him about my experience with God. Initially, he refused to provide proof and reiterated that the type of cancer that I had was not estrogen receptive and attempted to convince me of the need for treatment. He told me that it was impossible to prove the cancer was gone and assured me that the cancer was still there, but I insisted and was very persuasive, so he agreed to set up a Pep Scan. I took the Pep Scan on July 1, 2005 and was informed that the results would be available within 48 hours.

Two weeks later, I had not heard from the doctors' office. I was anxious, so I made the call to obtain my results. I was not worried because Jesus gave me peace through the dream.

Upon returning to the doctors' office I was greeted by a question that created a stir in my spirit. The doctor looked at me and asked "Did you have that surgery"? When I said no, a silence filled the room until I heard him say with astonishment, "there's nothing there". I knew that there was nothing there because Jesus took it at the cross. He healed me and I was free. I was free from intimidation and fear. Immediately, I jumped off the table and shouted, "I told you Jesus healed me". Thank you Lord for you unspeakable gift of salvation. I am cancer free because of what He did on Calvary.

Take some time now and begin to seek His face. You don't have to be a great Christian, you just need to have a desire to see Him as He reveals Himself to you. Don't worry about what you are going through. When God brings you out of the fire you won't even smell like smoke.

Dear heavenly father,

In the name of Jesus, I want to see You, I need to see you face to face. Lord, Please allow me to come to You now and behold the beauty of Your holiness. Let me see Your face as you breathe your breath of life into me. Lord, there is nobody like you and I am so thankful for what you have done for me. I am so thankful that I am receiving now Your healing power, I am receiving now the flow of the oil that comes from your presences. And I thank You as you Lord God increase great faith in me. Lord I bless you, Lord you are so good. You did not have to share this information with me, so God I praise you now. I love you so much. Lord I love you so much. Lord I love you so much. In Jesus name.

Amen

CHAPTER 11

YOU WILL NOT SMELL
LIKE SMOKE

"Well, look!" Nebuchadnezzar shouted. "I see four men, unbound, walking around in the fire, and they aren't even hurt by the flames! And the fourth looks like a god!"

Dan 3:25 (TLB)

JESUS will meet us in every trial we go through and bring us out without harm. I love what happened in the lives of the three Hebrew boys, when they made the decision to trust God. While Hananiah, Mishael, and Azariah were held captive in Babylon their names were changed to Shadrach, Meshach and Abednego, in order to glorify the god of the Babylonians. These men refused to dishonor God by worshipping the God of Nebuchadnezzar. Their fate was death in the fiery furnace, but God intervened and delivered them. Have you ever been in a house that has been on fire? There is a heavy smell of smoke that lingers in the air for days. The beautiful part about Gods intervention in our life is that we don't suffer any lose because of the trial we are going through. When we trust God we will come out of our trouble smelling like a rose. God met the boys in the fire, they weren't hurt, they did not die, and they didn't even smell like smoke. Besides this they had an opportunity to meet God "face to face" in the fire.

"He answered and said, Lo, I see four men loose, walking in the midst of the fire, and they have no hurt; and the form of the fourth is like the Son of God.

Dan 3:25

"Well, look!" Nebuchadnezzar shouted. "I see four men, unbound, walking around in the fire, and they aren't even hurt by the flames! And the fourth looks like a god!"

Dan 3:25 (TLB)

There isn't much that can compare to the gut wrenching feeling that you have when the doctor says "its cancer." Even the strongest person succumbs to the power of these words. It is unimaginable how a person can make it through this test without Jesus. The dread and depression that the word brings can devastate us more than the disease itself. Jesus was my only consolation and ray of hope, which caused me to seek Him with my whole heart.

Hananiah, Misheal and Azariah were cast into the fiery furnace, but God miraculously delivered them. The bible says that the fire didn't hurt them, their hair wasn't singed and they didn't even smell like smoke.

"And the princes, governors, and captains, and the king's counsellors, being gathered together, saw these men, upon whose bodies the fire had no power, nor was an hair of their head singed, neither were their coats changed, nor the smell of fire had passed on them.

Dan 3:27

LOOSED IN THE MIDST OF THE FIRE

In spite of the fact that the Hebrew boys were in the worst situation of their lives, they maintained their integrity and were freed in the midst of the fire. Jesus always shows up to help when we seek Him in our trouble.

The scripture clearly states that they were thrown into the fire bound but they were observed loose in the midst of the fire. No matter what your challenge, Jesus will set you free while you are going through it. The only requirement is to open your mouth and praise Him. Tell Him, thank you Jesus! Tell Him Jesus your great! Thank you Jesus. Thank you Jesus

> *"Now among these were of the children of Judah, Daniel, Hananiah, Mishael, and Azariah:"*
>
> *Dan 1:6*

It is significant that their birthright stemmed from the tribe of Judah, which means praises to God. They praised God in midst of trouble and pain. Praise coupled with an attitude of faith will secure what you need from God. Their attitude prior to being thrown into the furnace was of faith in God. They declared their lack of fear and confidence in Gods ability to deliver them from the flames when they decreed that they knew God was able.

> *"If it be so, our God whom we serve is able to deliver us from the burning fiery furnace, and he will deliver us out of thane hand, O king...*
>
> *Dan 3:17*

Again, Jesus reminds us that He will always be with us in times of trouble by showing up in the fire with us.

> *"Then Nebuchadnezzar the king was astonied, and rose up in haste, and spake, and said unto his counselors, Did not we cast three men bound into the midst of the fire? They answered and said unto the*

king, True, O king. He answered and said, Lo, I see four men loose,
walking in the midst of the fire, and they have no hurt; and the form
of the fourth is like the Son of God."

Dan 3:24-25

The key to maintaining the victory while in the fire is to surround
yourself with the truth. Begin a time of prayer and praise by telling God
that He is great. If you don't know what to say ask Him to tell you what
to say. Start with the following prayer:

Dear Jesus,
I praise You. I worship You and honor Your holy name. There is nobody
like You. You are the way the truth and my life. You are the great God
that brings me out of the fire at Your word and I bless you. Halleluiah!
Thank You Jesus! You are the King of Kings and the Lord of Lords and I
worship You.

CHAPTER 12

SURROUND YOURSELF WITH TRUTH

"Is any thing too hard for the LORD? At the time appointed I will return unto thee, according to the time of life, and Sarah shall have a son."

Gen 18:14

THE most important thing to remember when we are walking through life's trials is to surround our self with the truth. It is imperative that we surround ourselves with others that believe that God can do anything. God asked Abraham the question that we must all answer "Is there anything too hard for God."

It was nothing for God to cause a couple in their old age to conceive a child and it is certain that He is still moving on our behalf today. His purpose is fulfilled, and He heals us that He might prove to this generation that He is God.

Jeremiah also understood the awesome power of God. If we believe that He created heaven and earth, what can't He do? He can certainly heal these bodies that He made and bring all glory to His name. When faith causes Him to invade our world He touches us with His own hand. There is nothing too hard for Him. He is God!

"Ah Lord GOD! behold, thou hast made the heaven and the earth by thy great power and stretched out arm, and there is nothing too hard for thee:"

Jer 32:17

"Behold, I am the LORD, the God of all flesh: is there any thing too hard for me?"

Jer 32:27

"O Lord God! You have made the heavens and earth by your great power; nothing is too hard for you! You are loving and kind to thousands, yet children suffer for their fathers' sins; you are the great and mighty God, the Lord Almighty. You have all wisdom and do great and mighty miracles; for your eyes are open to all the ways of men, and you reward everyone according to his life and deeds. You have done incredible things in the land of Egypt-things still remembered to this day. And you have continued to do great miracles in Israel and all around the world. You have made your name very great, as it is today:"

Jer 32:17-20

His eyes are open to all the ways of men and He does great and mighty miracles as He continues to make His name great.

"But without faith it is impossible to please him: for he that cometh to God must believe that he is, and that he is a rewarder of them that diligently seek him."

Heb 11:6

"Sanctify them through thy truth: thy word is truth."

John 17:17

It is crucial to our victory that we surround ourselves with His word.

The greatest truth that we will ever come in contact with is the word of God. Study it, listen to it, read it, pray it, eat it, sleep it. He said in the Old Testament that He sent His word and healed us. Whatever He speaks shall surly come to pass. Hide His word in your heart in order to withdraw what you desire from a full account when you need it. His word is our medicine. It takes control of our circumstances and brings the desired result, our healing. After we consume and fill ourselves with His word we must then surround ourselves with those that are like minded. This is not the time to be in fellowship with unbelievers. The wrong relationships will chip away at your faith and cause you to waver. Well intentioned friends and family can cause you to lose your grip on God by their words. Faith exists when we believe Gods' word, while unbelief exists when we believe man's word. Shut out every other voice but the voice of your heavenly Father.

The first week after the diagnosis I decided that I wouldn't talk to anyone unless they had been healed of cancer. I was determined to find out how far they allowed the doctors to go and what God had spoken to them. I called Pastor Darlene Bishop who had a strong testimony about God's healing power and manifestation of the miraculous in her life. The words she spoke would prove to be another demarcation on the road to my healing. Her words of wisdom pushed me on and reconfirmed that I was doing the right thing by not returning to the doctor. She left a voice mail and said "you have nothing to fear but fear itself, so hold on to your confidence." Wow, nothing to fear but fear. We must hold onto our confidence and that confidence is in the Lord God. Trust Him no matter what you are facing. This was certainly a key to God's healing power. Fear destroys our faith. We can't have faith and fear at the same time. Again, the greatest promoter of fear and destruction of faith are the words of men. Concurrently, the greatest builder of faith is the Word of God. God's Word will heal us. Surround yourself with the truth. His word is truth.

Sanctify them through thy truth: thy word is truth. John 17:17

Take a moment now, pray this prayer and spend thirty minutes listening for His voice.

Heavenly Father,
I come to You at this very moment asking for Your faith. Please help me to shut out every other voice so that I can hear Your voice. You are the Master of this universe and the Healer of my body. Teach me to seek You diligently with all my heart and surround me with Your truth. Amen.

CHAPTER 13

WHAT MUST I DO TO BE HEALED?

"Bless the LORD, O my soul, and forget not all his benefits: Who forgiveth all thine iniquities; who healeth all thy diseases;"

Ps 103:2-3

A S we look to the Lord Jesus to heal us we must consider what he offers as a result of His death, burial, and resurrection at Calvary. Salvation is a free gift to all that will obey him. The word salvation means to be delivered preserved, protected, healed and or made whole. It is interesting that the name Jesus is a compound word that declares Jehovah is Salvation. The Lord God has become our salvation and as a result has loaded us up with benefits. God treats us well and gives us safety as a result of living for and obeying Him. Healing is one of the most exciting benefits of God and has been given in the package of salvation. When a man is saved and translated into the kingdom of God he becomes a partaker of all that God has. Healing, victory, prosperity and deliverance are all benefits of salvation.

'Blessed be the Lord, who daily loadeth us with benefits, even the God of our salvation. Selah. He that is our God is the God of salvation; and unto God the Lord belong the issues from death."

Ps 68:19-20

"Bless the LORD, O my soul, and forget not all his benefits: Who forgiveth all thine iniquities; who healeth all thy diseases;"

Ps 103:2-3

He wants to heal all of our diseases. He wants to bring us into a place of safety. Remission of sins is the corner stone of the gospel message to mankind, and the reason that Jesus shed His blood at Calvary. Over two thousand years ago in Jerusalem on the day of Pentecost, the New Testament church was founded and salvation was given to all that believed. Our sins are truly remitted because we believe in His word and act upon our belief.

"that they should repent and turn to God, and do works meet for repentance."

Acts 26:20

When I repented I began to think differently and reconsidered my path. In an instant, I evaluated my life of sin and rejected it for a new life with Jesus. I turned from myself and sin, and did an about face and ran to the Lord.

As we repent and turn to God we make the choice to enthusiastically submit to water baptism in His name.

"To him give all the prophets witness, that through his name whosoever believeth in him shall receive remission of sins."

Acts 10:43

"Then Peter said unto them, Repent, and be baptized every one of you in the name of Jesus Christ for the remission of sins, and ye shall receive the gift of the Holy Ghost."

Acts 2:38

According to Gods plan, we must repent, submit to water baptism in the name of the Lord Jesus and He will give us the gift of the Holy Ghost. This is Gods original and only plan for entering the Kingdom of God. As we obey and trust Him we are loaded with His benefits. The wonderful thing about salvation is that there are times that He gives the benefit of healing before we actually submit. It is during these occurrences that the joy over our healing will lead us to obey the Gospel of salvation.

Salvation is a process that begins with believing Gods word and repenting. Baptism in water and the infilling of His spirit will surely follow a repentant heart. I have prayed over this book and asked Jesus to send a minister of the Gospel to baptize you in Jesus name and that He would fill you up to overflowing with His spirit. As we do this our way of thinking changes to a God way of thinking.

As a result of repentance we have a new belief and change of mind that causes us to be buried with Jesus in the waters of baptism. As we come out of the water we are ready to walk in a brand new light. As a new citizen of the kingdom of God my mission has changed and I long for the things of God. I cannot get enough of His word and I cannot stop talking to Him in prayer. As a result of my transformation I praise Him every chance I get and I live my life according to His will.

There is a blessing for maintaining our faith in Him. We will be healed. We will be delivered and He will rescue us. Find someone to baptize you in water using the name of Jesus and then wait for a secret time to seek God and ask Him to baptize you in the Holy Ghost.

"If ye then, being evil, know how to give good gifts unto your children: how much more shall your heavenly Father give the Holy Spirit to them that ask him?"

Luke 11:13

Now that we understand salvation and its benefits let us pray to Jesus our Lord. The prayer of faith will heal the sick.

Dear Lord Jesus,
Make your word real in my life and give me the assurance of eternal life. You said that You would confirm your word with signs following. Give Me the sign that you have saved and rescued me. Give me Your salvation. Thank you.

CHAPTER 14

IT IS FINISHED
THE PRAYER OF FAITH

"And the prayer of faith shall save the sick, and the Lord shall raise him up; and if he have committed sins, they shall be forgiven him."

Jas 5:15

I believe that countless people would be healed if they understood God's plan for their healing. In the economy of God, healing is a covenantal promise. It is not a special gifting for the wise and powerful but a gift of faith available to all believers. Faith is not an easy thing to grasp when you are in the midst of the struggle but as we draw closer to Jesus we develop His ability to believe. We do not always believe God but in those times that we are overwhelmed with doubt His faith kicks in and supersedes our natural abilities. That is why we must believe His word and follow the instructions of our Lord. The Bible says "and the prayer of faith shall save the sick, and the Lord shall raise him up".

Faith is an inner work that causes us to have an attitude of believing God. It gives credence to the truth of God's words and persuades us that He is truthful, concerned and willing to make His word a reality in our life.

"And Jesus said unto them, Because of your unbelief: for verily I say unto you, If ye have faith as a grain of mustard seed, ye shall say unto

this mountain, Remove hence to yonder place; and it shall remove;
and nothing shall be impossible unto you."

Matt 17:20-21

Through faith we know that God can do anything in our life and the lives of others if we believe. Faith is a deep assurance that I can trust the Lord with my entire life and that He will bring us to the place that causes us to stand on His word.

The prayer of faith is a simple act of faith. I believe God and I pray in agreement with His word. It is not hard. It is easy. I pray in faith. I pray knowing that the Lord hears me and is willing and ready to answer my cry of faith. There is one prerequisite to praying in faith, forgiving. We are required to forgive and release ourselves and others to have a clear channel for the healing power of God. There are several areas of forgiveness that need to be covered as we cleanse ourselves and release God to heal us. We must forgive God, forgive ourselves, and forgive family and others that have offended us. You might say, I don't need to forgive God. Think about it. We hold God accountable for allowing the pain and sickness in our life and even ask why God would allow our sickness to happen to us. Remember that all things really do work together for our good if we love God.

"And Jesus answering saith unto them, Have faith in God. For verily
I say unto you, That whosoever shall say unto this mountain, Be thou
removed, and be thou cast into the sea; and shall not doubt in his
heart, but shall believe that those things which he saith shall come
to pass; he shall have whatsoever he saith. Therefore I say unto you,
What things so ever ye desire, when ye pray, believe that ye receive
them, and ye shall have them. And when ye stand praying, forgive, if
ye have ought against any: that your Father also which is in heaven
may forgive you your trespasses. But if ye do not forgive, neither will
your Father which is in heaven forgive your trespasses."

Mark 11:22-26

"And we know that all that happens to us is working for our good if we love God and are fitting into his plans."

Rom 8:28 (TLB)

In 1 Kings 2:21 Elijah stood on Mount Carmel and asked that life charging question, "how long hault ye between two opinions?" If God is God, believe Him. Is He God? Believe Him. After his confrontation with the prophets of Baal and the Grove, Elijah prayed the prayer of faith. He asked God to perform the miracle to prove to others that He was God. This is why Jesus wants to heal you. He wants to use your deliverance to prove to you, your family, the doctors and the heavenly host that He is God. We should note the components of Elijah's prayer:

"And it came to pass at the time of the offering of the evening sacrifice, that Elijah the prophet came near, and said, LORD God of Abraham, Isaac, and of Israel, let it be known this day that thou art God in Israel, and that I am thy servant, and that I have done all these things at thy word Hear me, O LORD, hear me, that this people may know that thou art the LORD God, and that thou hast turned their heart back again. Then the fire of the LORD fell, and consumed the burnt sacrifice, and the wood, and the stones, and the dust, and licked up the water that was in the trench. And when all the people saw it, they fell on their faces: and they said, The LORD, he is the God; the LORD, he is the God."

1 Kings 18:36-39 (KJV)

Elijah prayed let it be known that you are God. Jesus please receive the glory for this that the world may believe you. Let them know that I am your servant. As we pray in faith we must ask the Lord to prove to the world that we have not believed in vain and that He is with us.

Finally, Elijah asked that all of his actions would be attributed to his constant obedience and believing God.

We have experienced the healing power of God on numerous occasions over the years and have come to know that He is still healing His people. I have listed a few notable miracles that the Lord has shown us. I pray that your faith will be built and that you will receive your miracle also. A form has been provided at the end of this book for you to send us word of your healing. Please fill it out and send it to us so that we can rejoice with you. Jesus would like to add you to this list.

Miracle 1 - There was a woman that came to my home that was in the final stages of brain cancer. The tumor was inoperable and the doctors had given up all hope. The prognosis was that she had only four months to live. The first day that we met she made a statement that I will never forget. She said "I just want to stay here to watch my children grow up". Something inside me said "and you will". She came to my home that night and we prayed the prayer of faith over her asking God to save her and fill her with the Holy Ghost. Suddenly, she was filled with the Spirit of God and began to speak with other tongues. As she was rejoicing we took her outside to the swimming pool and baptized her in the name of the Lord. I remember feeling confused because between her tears and rejoicing, she kept saying that the pain was gone. We later learned that she never went through a day without excruciating pain from the tumor that caused constant headaches. We told her to go back to the hospital and have the doctor's check again for the tumor. The doctors were amazed and declared that the tumor was in remission. We knew that the Lord Jesus had healed her by His stripes. To God be the Glory!

Miracle 2 - A young women came to our ministry and was filled with the Holy Ghost and converted. She was in the final stages of leukemia and was given a few months to live by the doctors. While praying for her on the telephone God gave us another miracle. During the prayer I became ill with a painful stomach ache that incapacitated me for the duration of the day. It was hard for me to walk or to stand for any length of time. That night in revival the pain continued and seemed to get worse. The dear sister was in the congregation rejoicing because her pain was gone. She kept saying over and over again "you took away my pain". This woman had been in constant pain and had great difficulty walking and climbing the stairs but this particular night in the church service she began to run around the building, rejoicing and praising God for what He had done. It was at that moment that Jesus revealed to me how His wounds have healed us. Jesus takes our sickness and disease and bears it in His body. He takes our sickness in order for us to be free. The doctor wrote a letter to confirm this great miracle and said "I now believe in miracles if you believe." He could not find any abnormal blood cells. Glory to God!

> *But he was wounded for our transgressions, he was bruised for our iniquities: the chastisement of our peace was upon him; and with his stripes we are healed,*
>
> *Isa 53:5*

We have seen back problems caused by sciatic nerves healed, cancer healed, diabetes healed and deaf ears opened.

Miracle 3 - There was a woman that came to the retreat grounds with another church group that joined into the worship services with us. She asked us to pray for her baby. While praying for her baby, God filled her with His spirit and healed her child. The baby had been born deaf and couldn't hear out of her right ear. This elated mother began to rejoice and praise God because she knew immediately what God had done when the baby began to pull at her ear. She told us that she never touched her ear before because she couldn't hear out of it. After she left the retreat she took the baby to the doctor who confirmed that the ear was hearing.

Miracle 4 - In May of 2003, a certain woman came to our Women's

Conference. She had been beaten by her husband and hit in the head with the butt of his gun. As a result of this abuse her hair follicles were damaged and she lost ninety-five percent of her hearing in both ears. While we were worshiping God, He filled her with the Holy Ghost. As the women were rejoicing the noise was so loud that she took out her hearing aids. She is healed and can hear perfectly today.

Miracle 5 & 6 - In 2005, a woman was healed of a foot injury at her daughter's wedding and I was healed of cancer. Jesus is a wonder!

Miracle 7 - A woman was healed of Rheumatoid arthritis. There was a woman that came into our services that had debilitating arthritis. As we prayed the prayer of faith God healed her and she began to run around the building leaping and shouting.

The Bible says that the prayer of faith will heal the sick. You are not reading this book by accident. You are reading it by divine design. This was set up for you before the foundations of the earth. In His earthly ministry Jesus cried with tears because the people did not believe that He was with them to heal and deliver them. He is crying over you know. You are at the point of decision and you are about to take the leap of faith. Can I believe for my life you ask? Yes, you can. Open the packet of oil that is enclosed in this book and anoint your head with oil as a point of contact. Now pray the prayer of faith and receive your miracle.

Dear Lord Jesus,

I have been struggling for a long time and have tried everything that I know to find freedom from my sickness. The doctors cannot help and I turn to You with all of my heart. I am making a conscious decision to forgive everyone that has offended me and I call out each of their names know and give them to You. Lord, I forgive them and ask that You would forgive me for my offenses. I love You so much and trust You completely for my healing. Lord, prove to this generation that You are God. Show them that You can do the impossible that they might believe also and be free. I believe now that this infirmity in my flesh is being destroyed by You, by your word in response to my believing prayer. This disease is bowing the knee to the name of Jesus Christ. This sickness is destroyed by the power of Your word. I command it to go now, in the Name that is above every name, the name of the Lord Jesus Christ. Lord, I lift my hands to you I lift my heart to you God. I say yes and Amen to whatever you say. Lord, I thank you for the suffering that I have experienced. I thank you that you are establishing me and making me perfect. God I now believe that I can go through any situation. I can go thru any trial. I can go through any trouble. I even thank you for this sickness Lord that has caused me to come to you now with all my heart. Lord, I am praising you because you are good, I am praising you because you are wonderful, you are wonderful, you are a wonder. You are the living God. I praise you with all my heart. I give you thanks. I give you glory, I honor you. I ask you Lord to have your way in my life and to take out of me everything that is not of you. I give up Lord, I give up to you now and I say heal me God. I am ready to receive your healing oils in my life. I thank you now and I praise you in Jesus name. Amen Halleluiah Amen I praise you in Jesus name Amen Thank you for healing me.

HEALING SCRIPTURES IN THE BIBLE

READ and Meditate on the following scriptures. God's word is a Healing force.

Matt 4:23 And Jesus went about all Galilee, teaching in their synagogues, and preaching the gospel of the kingdom, and healing all manner of sickness and all manner of disease among the people.

Matt 9:35 And Jesus went about all the cities and villages, teaching in their synagogues, and preaching the gospel of the kingdom, and healing every sickness and every disease among the people.

Luke 9:6 And they departed, and went through the towns, preaching the gospel, and healing every where.

Luke 9:11 And the people, when they knew it, followed him: and he received them, and spake unto them of the kingdom of God, and healed them that had need of healing.

Acts 4:23 And being let go, they went to their own company, and reported all that the chief priests and elders had said unto them.

Acts 10:38 How God anointed Jesus of Nazareth with the Holy Ghost and with power: who went about doing good, and healing all that were oppressed of the devil; for God was with him.

Ex 15:26 And said, If thou wilt diligently hearken to the voice of the LORD thy God, and wilt do that which is right in his sight, and wilt give ear to his commandments, and keep all his statutes, I will put none of these diseases upon thee, which I have brought upon the Egyptians: for I am the LORD that healeth thee.

2 Chron 7:14 If my people, which are called by my name, shall humble themselves, and pray, and seek my face, and turn from their wicked ways; then will I hear from heaven, and will forgive their sin, and will heal their land.

Eccl 3:3 A time to kill, and a time to heal; a time to break down, and a time to build up;

Isa 19:22 And the LORD shall smite Egypt: he shall smite and heal it: and they shall return even to the LORD, and he shall be intreated of them, and shall heal them.

Isa 57:18 I have seen his ways, and will heal him: I will lead him also, and restore comforts unto him and to his mourners.

Isa 57:19 I create the fruit of the lips; Peace, peace to him that is far off, and to him that is near, saith the LORD; and I will heal him.

Jer 30:17 For I will restore health unto thee, and I will heal thee of thy wounds, saith the LORD; because they called thee an Outcast, saying, This is Zion, whom no man seeketh after.

Hosea 6:1 Come, and let us return unto the LORD: for he hath torn, and he will heal us; he hath smitten, and he will bind us up.

Matt 8:7 And Jesus saith unto him, I will come and heal him.

Matthew 10:1 And when he had called unto him his twelve disciples, he gave them power against unclean spirits, to cast them out, and to heal all manner of sickness and all manner of disease.

Matt 10:8 Heal the sick, cleanse the lepers, raise the dead, cast out devils: freely ye have received, freely give.

Matt 12:10-13
10 And, behold, there was a man which had his hand withered. And they asked him, saying, Is it lawful to heal on the sabbath days? that they might accuse him.
11 And he said unto them, What man shall there be among you, that shall have one sheep, and if it fall into a pit on the sabbath day, will he not lay hold on it, and lift it out?
12 How much then is a man better than a sheep? Wherefore it is lawful to do well on the sabbath days.
13 Then saith he to the man, Stretch forth thine hand. And he stretched it forth; and it was restored whole, like as the other.

Matt 13:15 For this people's heart is waxed gross, and their ears are dull of hearing, and their eyes they have closed; lest at any time they should see with their eyes, and hear with their ears, and should understand with their heart, and should be converted, and I should heal them.

Mark 3:14-15
14 And he ordained twelve, that they should be with him, and that he might send them forth to preach,
15 And to have power to heal sicknesses, and to cast out devils:

Luke 4:18 The Spirit of the Lord is upon me, because he hath anointed me to preach the gospel to the poor; he hath sent me to heal the brokenhearted, to preach deliverance to the captives, and recovering of sight to the blind, to set at liberty them that are bruised,

Luke 5:17 And it came to pass on a certain day, as he was teaching, that there were Pharisees and doctors of the law sitting by, which were come out of every town of Galilee, and Judaea, and Jerusalem: and the power of the Lord was present to heal them.

Luke 7:3 And when he heard of Jesus, he sent unto him the elders of the Jews, beseeching him that he would come and heal his servant.

Luke 9:1-2

9:1 Then he called his twelve disciples together, and gave them power and authority over all devils, and to cure diseases.

2 And he sent them to preach the kingdom of God, and to heal the sick.

Luke 10:8-9

8 And into whatsoever city ye enter, and they receive you, eat such things as are set before you:

9 And heal the sick that are therein, and say unto them, The kingdom of God is come nigh unto you.

John 4:47-54

47 When he heard that Jesus was come out of Judaea into Galilee, he went unto him, and besought him that he would come down, and heal his son: for he was at the point of death.

48 Then said Jesus unto him, Except ye see signs and wonders, ye will not believe.

49 The nobleman saith unto him, Sir, come down ere my child die.

50 Jesus saith unto him, Go thy way; thy son liveth. And the man believed the word that Jesus had spoken unto him, and he went his way.

51 And as he was now going down, his servants met him, and told him, saying, Thy son liveth.

52 Then inquired he of them the hour when he began to amend. And they said unto him, Yesterday at the seventh hour the fever left him.

33 So the father knew that it was at the same hour, in the which Jesus said unto him, Thy son liveth: and himself believed, and his whole house.

54 This is again the second miracle that Jesus did, when he was come out of Judaea into Galilee.

John 12:40 He hath blinded their eyes, and hardened their heart; that they should not see with their eyes, nor understand with their heart, and be converted, and I should heal them.

Acts 4:29-30

29 And now, Lord, behold their threatenings: and grant unto thy servants, that with all boldness they may speak thy word,

30 By stretching forth thine hand to heal; and that signs and wonders may be done by the name of thy holy child Jesus.

Acts 28:27 For the heart of this people is waxed gross, and their ears are dull of hearing, and their eyes have they closed; lest they should see with their eyes, and hear with their ears, and understand with their heart, and should be converted, and I should heal them.

Gen 20:17 So Abraham prayed unto God: and God healed Abimelech, and his wife, and his maidservants; and they bare children.

Matt 9:35 And Jesus went about all the cities and villages, teaching in their synagogues, and preaching the gospel of the kingdom, and healing every sickness and every disease among the people.

Luke 9:6 And they departed, and went through the towns, preaching the gospel, and healing every where.

Ps 103:2-3

2 Bless the LORD, O my soul, and forget not all his benefits:

3 Who forgiveth all thine iniquities; who healeth all thy diseases;

Ps 147:3 He healeth the broken in heart, and bindeth up their wounds.

Deut 32:39 See now that I, even I, am he, and there is no god with me: I kill, and I make alive; I wound, and I heal: neither is there any that can deliver out of my hand.

2 Kings 20:5 Turn again, and tell Hezekiah the captain of my people, Thus saith the LORD, the God of David thy father, I have heard thy prayer, I have seen thy tears: behold, I will heal thee: on the third day thou shalt go up unto the house of the LORD.

2 Kings 20:8-9
8 And Hezekiah said unto Isaiah, What shall be the sign that the LORD will heal me, and that I shall go up into the house of the LORD the third day?
9 And Isaiah said, This sign shalt thou have of the LORD, that the LORD will do the thing that he hath spoken: shall the shadow go forth ten degrees, or go back ten degrees?

Ps 30:1-3
I will extol thee, O LORD; for thou hast lifted me up, and hast not made my foes to rejoice over me.
2 O LORD my God, I cried unto thee, and thou hast healed me.
3 O LORD, thou hast brought up my soul from the grave: thou hast kept me alive, that I should not go down to the pit.

Ps 107:20-21
20 He sent his word, and healed them, and delivered them from their destructions.
21 Oh that men would praise the LORD for his goodness, and for his wonderful works to the children of men!

Isa 6:10 Make the heart of this people fat, and make their ears heavy, and shut their eyes; lest they see with their eyes, and hear with their ears, and understand with their heart, and convert, and be healed.

Ezek 47:9 And it shall come to pass, that every thing that liveth, which moveth, whithersoever the rivers shall come, shall live: and there shall be a very great multitude of fish, because these waters shall come thither: for they shall be healed; and every thing shall live whither the river cometh.

Matt 4:24 And his fame went throughout all Syria: and they brought unto him all sick people that were taken with divers diseases and torments, and those which were possessed with devils, and those which were lunatick, and those that had the palsy; and he healed them.

Matt 8:8 The centurion answered and said, Lord, I am not worthy that thou shouldest come under my roof: but speak the word only, and my servant shall be healed.

Matt 8:13 And Jesus said unto the centurion, Go thy way; and as thou hast believed, so be it done unto thee. And his servant was healed in the selfsame hour.

Matt 8:16 When the even was come, they brought unto him many that were possessed with devils: and he cast out the spirits with his word, and healed all that were sick:

Matt 12:15 But when Jesus knew it, he withdrew himself from thence: and great multitudes followed him, and he healed them all;

Matt 12:22 Then was brought unto him one possessed with a devil, blind, and dumb: and he healed him, insomuch that the blind and dumb both spake and saw.

Matt 14:14 And Jesus went forth, and saw a great multitude, and was moved with compassion toward them, and he healed their sick.

Matt 15:30-31
30 And great multitudes came unto him, having with them those that were lame, blind, dumb, maimed, and many others, and cast them down at Jesus' feet; and he healed them:
31 Insomuch that the multitude wondered, when they saw the dumb to speak, the maimed to be whole, the lame to walk, and the blind to see: and they glorified the God of Israel.

Matt 19:2 And great multitudes followed him; and he healed them there.

Matt 21:14 And the blind and the lame came to him in the temple; and he healed them.

Mark 1:34 And he healed many that were sick of divers diseases, and cast out many devils; and suffered not the devils to speak, because they knew him.

Mark 3:10 For he had healed many; insomuch that they pressed upon him for to touch him, as many as had plagues.

Mark 5:23 And besought him greatly, saying, My little daughter lieth at the point of death: I pray thee, come and lay thy hands on her, that she may be healed; and she shall live.

Mark 5:29 And straightway the fountain of her blood was dried up; and she felt in her body that she was healed of that plague.

Mark 6:5 And he could there do no mighty work, save that he laid his hands upon a few sick folk, and healed them.

Mark 6:13 And they cast out many devils, and anointed with oil many that were sick, and healed them.

Luke 4:40-41
40 Now when the sun was setting, all they that had any sick with divers diseases brought them unto him; and he laid his hands on every one of them, and healed them.
41 And devils also came out of many, crying out, and saying, Thou art Christ the Son of God. And he rebuking them suffered them not to speak: for they knew that he was Christ.

Luke 5:15 But so much the more went there a fame abroad of him: and great multitudes came together to hear, and to be healed by him of their infirmities.

Luke 6:17 And he came down with them, and stood in the plain, and the company of his disciples, and a great multitude of people out of all Judaea and Jerusalem, and from the sea coast of Tyre and Sidon, which came to hear him, and to be healed of their diseases;

Luke 6:18-19
18 And they that were vexed with unclean spirits: and they were healed.
19 And the whole multitude sought to touch him: for there went virtue out of him, and healed them all.

Luke 7:9-10
9 When Jesus heard these things, he marvelled at him, and turned him about, and said unto the people that followed him, I say unto you, I have not found so great faith, no, not in Israel.
10 And they that were sent, returning to the house, found the servant whole that had been sick.

Luke 8:2

2 And certain women, which had been healed of evil spirits and infirmities, Mary called Magdalene, out of whom went seven devils,

Luke 8:36 They also which saw it told them by what means he that was possessed of the devils was healed.

Luke 8:47 And when the woman saw that she was not hid, she came trembling, and falling down before him, she declared unto him before all the people for what cause she had touched him and how she was healed immediately.

Luke 9:42 And as he was yet a coming, the devil threw him down, and tare him. And Jesus rebuked the unclean spirit, and healed the child, and delivered him again to his father.

Luke 14:4 And they held their peace. And he took him, and healed him, and let him go;

Luke 17:15 And one of them, when he saw that he was healed, turned back, and with a loud voice glorified God,

Luke 22:51 And Jesus answered and said, Suffer ye thus far. And he touched his ear, and healed him.

John 5:6-8

6 When Jesus saw him lie, and knew that he had been now a long time in that case, he saith unto him, Wilt thou be made whole?

7 The impotent man answered him, Sir, I have no man, when the water is troubled, to put me into the pool: but while I am coming, another steppeth down before me.

8 Jesus saith unto him, Rise, take up thy bed, and walk.

Acts 3:11 And as the lame man which was healed held Peter and

John, all the people ran together unto them in the porch that is called Solomon's, greatly wondering.

Acts 4:14 And beholding the man which was healed standing with them, they could say nothing against it.

Acts 5:16 There came also a multitude out of the cities round about unto Jerusalem, bringing sick folks, and them which were vexed with unclean spirits: and they were healed every one.

Acts 8:7 For unclean spirits, crying with loud voice, came out of many that were possessed with them: and many taken with palsies, and that were lame, were healed.

Acts 14:9-10
9 The same heard Paul speak: who stedfastly beholding him, and perceiving that he had faith to be healed,
10 Said with a loud voice, Stand upright on thy feet. And he leaped and walked.

Acts 28:8 And it came to pass, that the father of Publius lay sick of a fever and of a bloody flux: to whom Paul entered in, and prayed, and laid his hands on him, and healed him.

Acts 28:9 So when this was done, others also, which had diseases in the island, came, and were healed:

James 5:16 Confess your faults one to another, and pray one for another, that ye may be healed. The effectual fervent prayer of a righteous man availeth much.

1 Peter 2:24 Who his own self bare our sins in his own body on the tree, that we, being dead to sins, should live unto righteousness: by whose stripes ye were healed.

Gods' Only Plan of Salvation—What Must I do to be Saved?

Four Steps

John 3:3-8 Jesus answered and said unto him, Verily, verily, I say unto thee, Except a man be born again, he cannot see the kingdom of God. Nicodemus saith unto him, How can a man be born when he is old? can he enter the second time into his mother's womb, and be born? Jesus answered, Verily, verily, I say unto thee, Except a man be born of water and of the Spirit, he cannot enter into the kingdom of God. That which is born of the flesh is flesh; and that which is born of the Spirit is spirit. Marvel not that I said unto thee, Ye must be born again. The wind bloweth where it listeth, and thou hearest the sound thereof, but canst not tell whence it cometh, and whither it goeth: so is every one that is born of the Spirit.

Acts 2:38-40 Then Peter said unto them, Repent, and be baptized every one of you in the name of Jesus Christ for the remission of sins, and ye shall receive the gift of the Holy Ghost. For the promise is unto you, and to your children, and to all that are afar off, even as many as the Lord our God shall call. And with many other words did he testify and exhort, saying, Save yourselves from this untoward generation.

Step One - Repent

Luke 24:47-49 And that repentance and remission of sins should be preached in his name among all nations, beginning at Jerusalem. And ye are witnesses of these things. And, behold, I send the promise of my Father upon you: but tarry ye in the city of Jerusalem, until ye be endued with power from on high.

Matt 3:2 And saying, Repent ye: for the kingdom of heaven is at hand.

Matt 3:8 Bring forth therefore fruits meet for repentance:

Matt 4:17 From that time Jesus began to preach, and to say, Repent: for the kingdom of heaven is at hand.

Luke 24:47 And that repentance and remission of sins should be preached in his name among all nations, beginning at Jerusalem.

Acts 3:19 Repent ye therefore, and be converted, that your sins may be blotted out, when the times of refreshing shall come from the presence of the Lord;

Acts 17:30 And the times of this ignorance God winked at; but now commandeth all men every where to repent:

Acts 20:21 Testifying both to the Jews, and also to the Greeks, repentance toward God, and faith toward our Lord Jesus Christ.

Acts 26:20 But shewed first unto them of Damascus, and at Jerusalem, and throughout all the coasts of Judaea, and then to the Gentiles, that they should repent and turn to God, and do works meet for repentance.

Step Two - Be Baptized in the Name of Jesus for the Remission of Sins

Acts 2:38-40 Then Peter said unto them, Repent, and be baptized every one of you in the name of Jesus Christ for the remission of sins, and ye shall receive the gift of the Holy Ghost. 39 For the promise is unto you, and to your children, and to all that are afar off, even as many as the Lord our God shall call. 40 And with many other words did he testify and exhort, saying, Save yourselves from this untoward generation.

Luke 24:47-49 And that repentance and remission of sins should be preached in his name among all nations, beginning at Jerusalem. And ye are witnesses of these things. And, behold, I send the promise of my Father upon you: but tarry ye in the city of Jerusalem, until ye be endued with power from on high.

Acts 8:12 But when they believed Philip preaching the things concerning the kingdom of God, and the name of Jesus Christ, they were baptized, both men and women.

Acts 8:16 (For as yet he was fallen upon none of them: only they were baptized in the name of the Lord Jesus.)

Acts 10:48 And he commanded them to be baptized in the name of the Lord. Then prayed they him to tarry certain days.

Acts 19:4 Then said Paul, John verily baptized with the baptism of repentance, saying unto the people, that they should believe on him which should come after him, that is, on Christ Jesus.

Rom 6:3 Know ye not, that so many of us as were baptized into Jesus Christ were baptized into his death?

1 Cor 1:13 Is Christ divided? was Paul crucified for you? or were ye baptized in the name of Paul?

Acts 8:36 And as they went on their way, they came unto a certain water: and the eunuch said, See, here is water; what doth hinder me to be baptized?

Acts 16:15 And when she was baptized, and her household, she besought us, saying, If ye have judged me to be faithful to the Lord, come into my house, and abide there. And she constrained us.

Acts 16:31 And they said, Believe on the Lord Jesus Christ, and thou shalt be saved, and thy house.

Acts 22:16 And now why tarriest thou? arise, and be baptized, and wash away thy sins, calling on the name of the Lord.

Titus 3:5 Not by works of righteousness which we have done, but according to his mercy he saved us, by the washing of regeneration, and renewing of the Holy Ghost;

1 Peter 3:21 The like figure whereunto even baptism doth also now save us (not the putting away of the filth of the flesh, but the answer of a good conscience toward God,) by the resurrection of Jesus Christ:

STEP THREE - GOD WILL FILL YOU WITH THE HOLY GHOST

Isa 32:15 Until the spirit be poured upon us from on high, and the wilderness be a fruitful field, and the fruitful field be counted for a forest.

Isa 44:3 For I will pour water upon him that is thirsty, and floods upon the dry ground: I will pour my spirit upon thy seed, and my blessing upon thine offspring:

Isa 59:21 21 As for me, this is my covenant with them, saith the LORD; My spirit that is upon thee, and my words which I have put in thy mouth, shall not depart out of thy mouth, nor out of the mouth of thy seed, nor out of the mouth of thy seed's seed, saith the LORD, from henceforth and for ever.

Ezek 36:25-27 Then will I sprinkle clean water upon you, and ye shall be clean: from all your filthiness, and from all your idols, will I cleanse you. A new heart also will I give you, and a new spirit will I put within you: and I will take away the stony heart out of your flesh, and I will give you an heart of flesh. And I will put my spirit within you, and cause you to walk in my statutes, and ye shall keep my judgments, and do them.

Ezek 39:29 Neither will I hide my face any more from them: for I have poured out my spirit upon the house of Israel, saith the Lord GOD.

Joel 2:28-29 28 And it shall come to pass afterward, that I will pour out my spirit upon all flesh; and your sons and your daughters shall prophesy, your old men shall dream dreams, your young men shall see visions: 29 And also upon the servants and upon the handmaids in those days will I pour out my spirit.

Acts 2:16-18 But this is that which was spoken by the prophet Joel; And it shall come to pass in the last days, saith God, I will pour out of my Spirit upon all flesh: and your sons and your daughters shall prophesy, and your young men shall see visions, and your old men shall dream dreams: 18 And on my servants and on my handmaidens I will pour out in those days of my Spirit; and they shall prophesy:

Acts 8:15-17 Who, when they were come down, prayed for them, that they might receive the Holy Ghost: (For as yet he was fallen upon none of them: only they were baptized in the name of the Lord Jesus.) Then laid they their hands on them, and they received the Holy Ghost.

Acts 10:44-46 While Peter yet spake these words, the Holy Ghost fell on all them which heard the word. And they of the circumcision which believed were astonished, as many as came with Peter, because that on the Gentiles also was poured out the gift of the Holy Ghost. For they heard them speak with tongues, and magnify God. Then answered Peter,

Acts 19:2-6 He said unto them, Have ye received the Holy Ghost since ye believed? And they said unto him, We have not so much as heard whether there be any Holy Ghost. And he said unto them, Unto what then were ye baptized? And they said, Unto John's baptism. Then said Paul, John verily baptized with the baptism of repentance, saying unto the people, that they should believe on him which should come after him, that is, on Christ Jesus. When they heard this, they were baptized in the name of the Lord Jesus. And when Paul had laid his hands upon them, the Holy Ghost came on them; and they spake with tongues, and prophesied.

Step Four - Live a Holy and Sanctified Life before the Lord

Gal 5:24-25 And they that are Christ's have crucified the flesh with the affections and lusts. If we live in the Spirit, let us also walk in the Spirit.

John 6:63 It is the spirit that quickeneth; the flesh profiteth nothing: the words that I speak unto you, they are spirit, and they are life.

Rom 8:2 For the law of the Spirit of life in Christ Jesus hath made me free from the law of sin and death.

Rom 8:10 And if Christ be in you, the body is dead because of sin; but the Spirit is life because of righteousness.

2 Cor 3:6 Who also hath made us able ministers of the new testament; not of the letter, but of the spirit: for the letter killeth, but the spirit giveth life.

1 Peter 4:6 For for this cause was the gospel preached also to them that are dead, that they might be judged according to men in the flesh, but live according to God in the spirit.

Rom 8:4-5 That the righteousness of the law might be fulfilled in us, who walk not after the flesh, but after the Spirit. For they that are after the flesh do mind the things of the flesh; but they that are after the Spirit the things of the Spirit.

Gal 5:16-18 This I say then, Walk in the Spirit, and ye shall not fulfil the lust of the flesh. For the flesh lusteth against the Spirit, and the Spirit against the flesh: and these are contrary the one to the other:

so that ye cannot do the things that ye would. But if ye be led of the Spirit, ye are not under the law.

Rom 6:19 I speak after the manner of men because of the infirmity of your flesh: for as ye have yielded your members servants to uncleanness and to iniquity unto iniquity; even so now yield your members servants to righteousness unto holiness.

Rom 6:22 But now being made free from sin, and become servants to God, ye have your fruit unto holiness, and the end everlasting life.

2 Corinthians 7:1 Having therefore these promises, dearly beloved, let us cleanse ourselves from all filthiness of the flesh and spirit, perfecting holiness in the fear of God.

Eph 4:24 And that ye put on the new man, which after God is created in righteousness and true holiness.

1 Thess 3:13 To the end he may stablish your hearts unblameable in holiness before God, even our Father, at the coming of our Lord Jesus Christ with all his saints.

1 Thess 4:7 For God hath not called us unto uncleanness, but unto holiness.

Titus 2:3 The aged women likewise, that they be in behaviour as becometh holiness, not false accusers, not given to much wine, teachers of good things;

Heb 12:10 For they verily for a few days chastened us after their own pleasure; but he for our profit, that we might be partakers of his holiness.

Heb 12:14 Follow peace with all men, and holiness, without which no man shall see the Lord:

I want to hear about your results after reading this book. Please send me your Praise report.

Praise Report

I was healed from _____

_____

My Testimonial is _____

_____

You may contact me at: _____

_____

Mail:

Roxane Harper
793 S Tracy Blvd #290
Tracy, CA 95376

Email: healingoils@culturemg.com

I want to hear about your results after reading this book. Please send me your Praise report.

PRAISE REPORT

I was healed from _____

_____

My Testimonial is _____

_____

You may contact me at: _____

_____

Mail:

Roxane Harper
793 S Tracy Blvd #290
Tracy, CA 95376

Email: healingoils@culturemg.com

NOTES

NOTES

OIL PACKET

Use this Oil when Praying the Prayer of Faith